finding
serenity
in seasons
of stress

finding
serenity
in seasons
of stress

simple solutions for difficult times

Candy Paull

GRAND
HARBOR
PRESS

Published by Grand Harbor Press
1704 Eaton Drive
Grand Haven, MI 49417

ISBN-13: 9781477848111
ISBN-10: 1477848118

Library of Congress Control Number: 2013940848

Printed in the United States of America

Dedicated to my readers:

We meet in the Secret Place of the Most High

From listening to your body to hearing the still, small intuitive voice in your heart, it is my prayer that *Finding Serenity in Seasons of Stress* will help you find both spiritual and practical inspiration that will not only make your day better, but introduce you to the deepest part of yourself—the true heart that is sacred, serene, and beautiful at all times.

—Candy Paull

Contents

With an eye made quiet by the power of harmony, and the deep power of joy, we see into the life of things.
—William Wordsworth

Stress is the perception that we are separated from our divine source.
—Brian Luke Seaward

Introduction

*The serene, silent beauty of a holy life is the most powerful influence in
the world, next to the might of the Spirit of God.*
—Blaise Pascal

Serenity. You hear it in the music of Debussy, Mozart, Bach,
and Brahms—a smooth flow of melody and harmony that
soothes your heart and calms your mind. Or you might find it
in the achingly beautiful *Quiet City* by Aaron Copland, or in the
sound of a flute played in the abstract beauty of a Japanese garden.
Serenity is a picture of a beautiful meadow with horses grazing
and grass as green as a four-leaf clover, or a tranquil lake mirror-
ing a cloudless azure sky. You sense it in the old masters' paintings
of Mary, with her sweet smile and tranquil expression, or in the
mysterious smile of Leonardo da Vinci's *Mona Lisa*. Serenity is
the sigh of relief as you sink into bed after a long busy day, or the
feeling of release in the aftermath of a storm of tears.

Yet in our frazzled society, serenity is hard to find. You look
in the mirror, but instead of a serene, smiling face, you see your
own worried countenance. How do you achieve serenity in this
ever-accelerating modern age? How can you find the stillness
and tranquility that brings a higher perspective on life and your
place in it?

The solution doesn't have to be complex, and you don't have to rearrange your entire life. Cultivating inner serenity can begin with small adjustments that will shift your attention and move you into a calmer place. Serenity is a gift that comes moment by moment, choice by choice. It grows from within and expands outwardly. Serenity can exist in the midst of a storm, as well as when the sun shines in a cloudless sky. *Finding Serenity in Seasons of Stress* offers thoughts that help you tap into that higher, more spiritual viewpoint; yet it attends to the earthy details and simple choices that enable you to create the life of your dreams instead of the drama of your nightmares.

Finding Serenity in Seasons of Stress offers a combination of practical help and spiritual insight to help you bridge the gap between the way things are and the way you wish they could be. There are no guarantees or promises of nirvana, just simple suggestions for coping with the stress of daily life and thoughts that might inspire you to find a higher perspective during troublesome times. You'll find practical ideas for body, mind, and spirit that will help you cope with unavoidable stress and inspire you to eliminate that which no longer serves you. With small adjustments to seemingly minor stress points, you can learn to simplify your life and make room for more beauty, meaning, and joy. You'll be reminded of things you already know but often forget when the pressures of life become overwhelming.

From commonsense advice you've heard for years from mothers, mentors, and teachers, to heartfelt thoughts about what it means to make the choices that soften the hard blows life can deliver, *Finding Serenity in Seasons of Stress* was written to help you discover reminders of hope and encouragement for the soul in any season of life. Created to inspire you in the midst of a busy life, this book not only addresses the outward symptoms of stress and tension, but also encourages you to examine the root causes, which are spiritual in nature.

Filled with simple suggestions for making life just a bit calmer and more ordered, *Finding Serenity in Seasons of Stress* offers an antidote to the frustration and stress of everyday living. Let these pages be an oasis in the middle of a busy day—a reminder of your own capacity for healing and beauty, and an exploration of new possibilities for leading a more tranquil and spiritually expansive existence.

This collection of ideas is a gentle reminder of the wisdom you already carry within. It is a reminder that there is Something wiser and more benevolent at work in the circumstances and conditions of your life, and Someone who loves you without judgment or condemnation—no matter how you may feel you have failed to live up to your God-given potential. You are not bound by the history of your past, the limits of your understanding. There is a core of serenity—an inner guidance system that resides in your heart and expresses in your soul. This is the place where love begins, and it is your true nature, your authentic self beneath all the masks of personality, ego, and the small self that clings and clutches.

May you make a simple choice to become more aware and to cultivate a serene spirit. This is the starting place for an inner revolution that can color your entire life with light, joy, love, and a sense of peace and plenitude. Open your heart to accept the sweet serenity that is always at the center of your being.

If there is light in the soul,
There will be beauty in the person.
If there is beauty in the person,
There will be harmony in the house.
If there is harmony in the house,
There will be order in the nation.
If there is order in the nation,
There will be peace in the world.
—Chinese proverb

part one

The Heart of Serenity

Man ordinarily goes no further than his own experience (and that includes the experience of the race) for help in an emergency. But those who go still further within themselves for the answer will find a timeless wisdom and inspiration to be translated into the human need of the moment.

—Letters of the Scattered Brotherhood

chapter one

Serenity Is a Choice

We have to make peace and reduce the suffering in ourselves first, because we represent the world. Peace, love, and happiness must always begin here, with ourselves. There is suffering, fear, and anger inside of us, and when we take care of it, we are taking care of the world. . . . So first you have to focus on the practice of being. Being fresh. Being peaceful. Being attentive. Being generous. Being compassionate.
—Thich Nhat Hanh

It was a cold November night, and my birthday. I knew I would be alone that evening, and my usual choice would have been to sink into a funk or watch television. But for once, I decided to do something special, a little different. I decided to attend a meditation at Nashville Mindfulness Center. I had gone to two meditation services with a friend, both special occasions with singing bowl ceremonies that had left me feeling peaceful and my whole body vibrating with calm energy. Tonight I would be going by myself, and it would be a regular meditation night with no special ceremonies or larger-than-usual crowds.

I walked up the steps that led to a massive wooden door and entered shyly. It was quiet with candles burning and a serene atmosphere. The director welcomed me warmly. He offered simple instructions in how to sit on the meditation cushion, what to expect during the meditation time, and a brief story about how he had studied with Thich Nhat Hanh—the Vietnamese monk who is one of the most beloved Buddhist teachers in the West. The meditation leader, who had converted the solarium of his home into a meditation center, had been ordained in Thich Nhat Hanh's order and led meditation every week. That night, I was introduced to mindfulness meditation, and it began a two-year journey into the power and healing of meditative practice.

Week after week I would return to the meditation and find peace and release. I learned to let go of my jumbled thoughts, to breathe in and to breathe out, to be totally focused in the moment. I released the difficulties and stresses of my life, which were the most challenging I had ever experienced. I was fighting to keep my home, struggling with a financial meltdown, watching my career disintegrate, and feeling frightened and bewildered most of the time. This time of meditation became more and more important, as essential as food and air. I breathed in serenity and breathed out all the fear. Those two hours every Wednesday night became a lifeline as I faced bill collectors, foreclosure notices, health issues, and the end of life as I had known it.

The habit of meditation became an important part of my day, helping me stop the cold sweat of fear at two in the morning and go back to sleep, or calm down when yet another unexpected crisis arose. I learned to cultivate serenity not only by choosing my thoughts, but also by training my body to release fear and tension. Though the meditation center has closed and my meditation teacher has moved away, I still practice the lessons

I learned and meditate to continue cultivating serenity in all the seasons of my life. Meditation has helped me reinvent my life, enhancing my ability to cope with stress and helping me integrate spiritual practice and practical living in a deeper and more satisfying way. It has taught me that serenity is available to us on a moment-by-moment basis. It is the essence of life, beating as steadily as my heart, hidden beneath all the changing circumstances I experience. I have learned how practicing serenity in times of stress can help me sense a deep, intuitive wisdom that has helped me survive—and even thrive—in the midst of turbulent times.

Think of a moment when you felt exquisitely alive—the kind of moment you wished would last forever: standing by a magnificent waterfall, trembling on the edge of a first kiss, sleeping under the stars, being immersed in a project or sport, gazing out on an expansive horizon from a mountaintop, soaking in the glory of a red and purple and gold sunset. Contrast that to moments when you're caught in the insanity of rush hour traffic, a workday morning when you're running late, a hurried lunch so you can get a dozen papers off your desk, and a frazzled evening doing laundry and paying bills. Serenity comes when you stop and give undivided attention to what *is,* allowing you to experience an exquisite deep peace that helps you relax inside and move into harmony with your heart.

The Difference between Stress and Serenity

When you are relaxed and serene, your energy is focused, you can think more clearly, and you are able to organize your thoughts more effectively. You live harmoniously in body, mind, and spirit. Like a cloudless sky reflected in a limpid pool, even the very air you breathe imparts a soothing atmosphere. But most days feel more like stormy seas, with stress and emotional upheaval, swinging moods, and clamoring deadlines. Financial issues, upsetting headlines, and stress at work or school can rob you of serenity, leaving you exhausted and drained. Relationships get tangled, nerves get jangled, and the serene clarity you experienced in a morning's meditation gets overwhelmed by an afternoon of crisis and calamity. And this may be on a good day!

Here's an illustration of what stress can do—and how making a simple, subtle change can relieve stress and make life easier. Place a small rock in the open palm of your hand. Now clench your fist around that rock, holding it tightly, keeping your muscles rigid and tense. How long can you hold this position comfortably? Notice how quickly your hand tires. If you hold this position for too long, your hand becomes stiff and painful, and that rigidity spreads to your entire body. Now open your hand again, allowing the rock to lie comfortably in the center of your open palm. Hold it softly, open, still, and quiet. Do you think you could hold the rock more comfortably for a longer period of time in this open position?

How often have you clutched your life in a clenched fist, fighting the natural forces, trying to control and confine life within the small boundaries of your fears and expectations? It is as uncomfortable for the human heart to be clenched and closed as it is for the human hand. Stress is a hand grasping and clutching. Serenity is an open hand ready to receive the gifts life has to offer and to release that which no longer serves. Serenity is choosing to believe in Something Greater than the limits that our life conditions would indicate. Finding serenity is less about keeping your outer life under control and more about anchoring your reality in the unseen of the spiritual realm. There is a Higher Power and an inner wisdom that can offer you peace in the midst of a storm. Cultivating that interior life can transform you from the inside out.

Cultivating serenity allows you to experience the life force moving through you and to tap into the essence of your own being. When you are in a place of stillness and serenity, everything becomes clear and you gain a more detached and higher perspective of whatever situation you are experiencing. As muddy water in a glass settles and clears with patient waiting, so do your mind and emotions settle and clarify when you choose to practice inner stillness. Choosing to focus on each moment with quiet awareness, you are more able to respond appropriately and make fully conscious choices instead of allowing yourself to be driven by unconscious forces.

Choose Your Attitude

How you think about your life can make a difference in how you experience life. If you always focus on what you don't have and what is wrong, you will create more stress through your frustration and negativity. Instead, choose to focus on what's right and good in your life. A positive mind-set helps you develop a lighter, happier attitude that cushions the bumps in the road.

So often we are frazzled because we have overextended ourselves. We are out of temper because we try to do too much, set unrealistic standards of performance for ourselves and others, try to control and predict every outcome, and generally try to stuff too much into our lives. We then beat ourselves up for not having instant peace and wisdom and wonder why we are so tired, angry, and frustrated. God wants to give us the gift of serenity, stillness, and quiet wisdom if we would only stop long enough to allow him to do so.

*It is only a question of whether you will allow yourself to be ordinary,
and to do what comes naturally to you, and what seems most sensible,
to your heart, always to your heart, not to the images which false learn-
ing has coated on your mind.*
—Christopher Alexander

You can find inner serenity no matter what your circum-
stances are, for serenity is tied to what is happening within you,
not what is going on all around you. You may find serenity by
gazing at a lighted candle, opening the door of a newly ordered
closet, or by making a clear commitment to honoring your
own truth. Simple ideas for a practical spirituality—or a spiri-
tual practicality—help you create an island of serenity in a sea of
chaos. As you anchor yourself to a serenity that begins within, it
eventually affects the outer conditions of your life.

Making More Conscious Choices

Our lives reflect who we are and what we have allowed our-
selves to become. We do not become more serene by chance
but by choice. The only difference between those who have
control of their destiny and those who feel controlled by events
is how conscious they are of the choices they make. If we make
choices unconsciously, moved by a reaction to outer circum-
stances or driven by our own random and chaotic thoughts,
we have habituated ourselves to being constrained in a mental
prison created by our own lack of understanding.

We have often chosen without knowing we had a choice. We
assume that life controls us, that we are victims of circumstance.
But it is our choices that lead us step by step into the circum-
stances in which we find ourselves. We sometimes drift with the
tide and run aground on the rocks, choosing by not choosing.
We must consciously steer the vessels of our lives in another and

more fulfilling direction. We constantly make choices, and each choice has its consequence, which leads to more choices and more consequences. Most people are so unaware of their own choices that they never realize they had made a decision and never recognize that the chain of causation was set in motion by their own unconscious assumptions.

For instance, it's easy to react automatically to a negative situation and replay old victim stories with a new cast of characters, even when the new situation has nothing to do with the situations of the past. Perhaps someone betrayed us in the past, and when confronted with a new hurtful situation, we assume that we have been betrayed again. What has happened before seems to be happening again, and so we fall into the same patterns of behavior without thinking.

The first step toward serenity is recognizing that you are replaying an old script in a new situation. Observing without judgment is a powerful way to gain better perspective. With this perspective, you are able to make a more conscious choice to respond to a negative situation in a more positive way—you empower yourself and become a responsible actor in the scenario instead of limiting yourself to old, childish patterns.

Feeling powerless is one factor that contributes to our perception of life as being stressful. Modern society is built around concepts of power that make us feel our individual choices are meaningless. A traffic jam on the way to work, an arbitrary supervisor who thwarts our best efforts, the impersonal bureaucratic red tape that complicates even the simplest task, a system of government that increasingly favors the rich and penalizes the poor, or a family system of enablement and denial all seem to trap us into negative-feedback loops that pull us into pointless tail chasing. We can get caught in our own limiting cycle of poor choices, dooming us to forever repeat the same mistakes. One definition of craziness is doing the same thing over and over, expecting different results. Our attempts to control results or overcome negative systems are often frustrating attempts to force change from the outside, and they end up reinforcing the negative-feedback loops. What we resist persists.

However, small, incremental choices that come from a positive sense of authenticity and meaning can create a renewed and vibrant experience. Choosing to see the truth that is beyond mere fact and condition exerts a subtle influence that can lead to consequences in ways we cannot imagine. Chaos theory tells us that a change as subtle as the movement of a butterfly wing can affect the formation of a storm on the other side of the globe.

You cannot predict how or when or even if your choices will change the world, but a new thought and a different choice will certainly help you begin to see beyond a current belief structure and past experience. You can choose to move beyond your own outdated boundaries and limited context to create a more intelligent response to a challenging situation. In doing so, you will open yourself up to new possibilities.

Choices are the hinges of destiny.
—Edwin Markham

Rosa Parks had been working to challenge the power structure of segregation in Alabama for many years. But it was her decision on December 1, 1955, to refuse to give up her seat on a Montgomery bus that was the spark that started a revolution. The civil rights movement was already in motion, but her choice that day was unexpectedly magnified by the response of others to her act of courage. It started the historic 381-day boycott of Montgomery buses and fueled a movement that lead to the 1956 US Supreme Court ruling that segregation is unconstitutional.

Your choices may not influence the consciousness of a nation in such a dramatic way, but you can never predict the complexity of influences a single choice can affect. You can be sure that making better, more authentic choices over time will affect the trajectory of your life in positive ways. One small victory, one affirmative choice to express the highest integrity can exert a subtle influence far larger than the moment would indicate.

Choice is the nature of human free will. Even in the most constrained circumstances we are making choices. One person may choose to give up and play the victim's role, making an unconscious choice to say no to his own destiny and greatness. Another may make a different choice; conscious of the consequences, committed to following through on the links in the chain of causation to a larger and more spacious outcome. The victim gives up before he even begins; the one who chooses with greater consciousness becomes a cocreator with God, exercising his power and potential in a new way. It is not a question of whether we make choices; we make them all the time. It is a question of whether or not we are making those choices consciously.

Once you realize that you are the chooser and become more aware of your decisions, you discover that you are not only creating new options, you are also developing better character. You open the door to becoming more than you were before you made your choice. Because you have started to take responsibility and claim your power to choose consciously, a new skill and understanding will grow and flourish within your heart and soul.

Small, incremental choices can change the trajectory of a life. No longer a slave to your past or to the popular assumptions of your era, you become maker and creator of the world you inhabit. Conscious choices develop your character as much as they develop the circumstances that unfold in your life. Making a conscious choice is a way to be proactive for your own good. Like the ripples ringing where a stone was tossed into the surface of a still pond, your conscious choice carries a circle of consequences that expands beyond the impact of a single choice. To choose consciously and positively is to say yes to your own destiny.

A Higher Good

Every time you make a more conscious choice for a higher good, you will draw even greater good into your life. When you consistently make choices that create calm and peace, you develop a more serene way of dealing with the challenges and changes that life brings.

Set your intentions for the good, aim toward wholeness and health, and you will be aligning yourself with the natural forces of the universe. This is the true meaning of being "in the will of God." It is not a forced decision against your own nature but a recognition that the harmony and order of all of creation is in tune with the love of God, and you are meant to be a part of that beautiful music. God is love, and so are you. Choose to live in that love, and allow the loving nature of God to express itself in all facets of your life.

Seek Spiritual Solutions

There is a spiritual root to every problem in your life. The outer situation points to an inner struggle within you. Even when a problem seems to be caused by a person or situation that is out of your control, your response is a spiritual response. Set aside a time to pray and meditate on a specific issue that has been bothering you. Make a commitment to listen to your inner voice, and then to act on the wisdom you receive.

You will discover that when you cease resisting the good and allow it to flow in your life, the very goodness and greatness of the nature of creation will respond, leading you and even carrying you in unexpected ways to ever greater good. Synchronicity, or Divine timing, will appear more frequently in your life, bringing resources, people, events, and opportunities together in ways that may sometimes feel miraculous. The law of attraction will begin to work in your favor instead of against you.

But even more, you will discover that continued conscious choices made in favor of service and goodness will create an unforeseen yet entirely natural consequence: a transformed character. Anger is replaced by forgiveness and patience. Victimhood becomes unexpected strength to overcome difficult circumstances. Erratic behavior turns into a steady ability to persevere. Calmness and common sense temper impulsiveness and passion. This doesn't happen overnight. But the changes, once begun, have their own momentum. Your small daily choices grow into life patterns. Whereas once you were chained by unproductive habits, you discover your power to replace those habits with those that serve you better. As you release the old habits that no longer serve you, room is made for the new good that supports and sustains you.

Instead of allowing yourself to feel like a victim of circumstances, take responsibility for your own actions. Even if you are not in a situation by choice, you still have choice within the situation. You do have more power than you realize, and access to Divine wisdom. You have the power to change your circumstances, starting with what you think, then taking inspired action based on inner wisdom.

Today is the only day you have to make a choice. Yesterday is past, and you live in the consequences of the choices that were made back then. Tomorrow will manifest the consequences of the choices you make today. You choose your future in the here and now. You do this one thought at a time, one decision at a time, one action at a time. The eternal part of you that is connected to God is always and only available in the here and now. It is the part of you that knows only this moment as an eternal moment.

Make a conscious decision to cultivate serenity in your life. Take one small positive action toward the serene life you visualize. Then trust that Divine processes and rhythms are at work, just as the process of a storm finally blows itself out until the sun breaks through the clouds again. There is a river of life flowing in and through you. Instead of resisting the flow of life, align yourself with it. Then let this harmonious and Divine orderly flow lead you to vistas of freedom and love that are beyond anything you could have imagined.

You can make choices that come from the serenity of the heart instead of the urgency of the world around you. A single choice that honors the spirit can be more powerful than a hundred decisions that are motivated by outer circumstances. It can affect the quality of your day and have a lasting impact on the rest of your life.

Activity: Transform Your Thinking

What does it mean to transform your thinking? One way is to become aware of your thoughts and actively choose to think better thoughts. Get out of a negative mental rut and decide to think about higher things. Stop going over why things went wrong or how someone hurt you. Choose to move from negative thoughts to more positive and creative thoughts. Replace complaints with praise. Take it easy on yourself. Be compassionate to others. Remember that everyone is doing the best they can with what they understand at the time. Give yourself room to grow. Believe that a Higher Power is helping others to grow, too. Give the gift of compassionate grace and let love have the last word. It's your willingness to practice a positive faith that overcomes your fears and doubts. Optimism strengthens faith. Negativity saps energy and often creates the very thing you dread. When you find yourself thinking negatively, create a positive affirmation to replace the negative talk. Allow the light of love to transform your thoughts.

Three Affirmations

- I love life and I bring my best self to life.
- I am guided every step of the way, every moment of the day.
- I release all my egotistical agendas and live freely, joyously, and naturally.

chapter two

Coming Home to Serenity

The specific patterns out of which a building or a town is made may be alive or dead. To the extent they are alive, they let our inner forces loose, and set us free; but when they are dead, they keep us locked in inner conflict.
—Christopher Alexander

Somewhere between the conformities of an outdated fundamentalism and the lonely emptiness of unbelief, I have been forging a practical mysticism that works for me. If you are willing to forgo your own attachment to old ideas and skepticism, I would like to offer some new thoughts—a few small adjustments that could help change the trajectory of your life.

We are experiencing a paradigm shift of monumental proportions. People in every era believe they live in times of chaos and transition, but today there is a consensus that these truly are transformative times. Our institutions are inadequate to meet the challenges of the twenty-first century and must be reinvented and reimagined. Political gridlock, financial meltdowns, global climate change, technological innovations, and changes in the belief systems that once seemed so foundational are all part of a shift from the Cartesian/Newtonian worldview to a more integrative worldview. Every discipline is experiencing a shift in perspective. Art, architecture, social sciences, economics, governments, businesses, religions, and more are changing. If you are feeling more stress, it's not just because of the usual pace of technological and social change; it is truly a global crisis that affects us all, demanding new skills and a more expanded understanding of the way things work. The worldview of life as inert matter that can be separated into parts is transforming into a worldview of everything being connected and alive.

New solutions and more effective approaches emerge with a new paradigm. You have the choice to embrace your own paradigm shift. You can move from being hypnotized by what happens in the material world (the outer conditions of your life) to discovering that consciousness is the primary cause behind everything, and you can make more-conscious choices to affect change in the material world. Your attitudes, beliefs, and actions can create a better reality. Instead of looking at the visible and assuming that the conditions that exist are set in stone, you can consciously connect to the invisible as the source of all change. All that is visible and seems most solid and "real" is actually energy and space flowing from the invisible realm. A spiritual awakening offers you the opportunity to reinvent your own paradigm, liberating you from old limiting beliefs. Shift your worldview and create a new world.

New paradigms do not emerge suddenly in complete form and full power. They are often birthed in fits and starts. Challenges and confusion are the birth pangs of a new world being born, whether in the global community or in your personal life. The rules are being changed, and you have to change, too. The connections between choice and consequences are not always clear-cut or obvious. It is only by looking back later that you can see a new pattern was emerging from the chaos and changes of life.

The initial reason for change may have been to alleviate stress or to solve a problem, but it can eventually lead to new vistas of opportunity and possibility. We make our choices, and our choices, in the end, make us. It is a grand adventure to enter into a more intuitive and organic experience of reality. You may think you are finding some simple solutions for stress relief, but you are actually opening yourself to the possibility of personal transformation.

Create a Sacred Center

It is always your choice either to go more deeply into an experiment in transformation or to resist and hold back. Gentle, authentic, loving choices grow a new sense of awareness incrementally, helping you become more at home in a universe that includes safety as well as expansion. Coming home to yourself includes creating a container for growth and experimentation. We carry an eternal home within, and we create spaces in our physical homes to stay in touch with that inner home.

There is a sacred center, a ground of being, a hidden spring within our hearts that flows ever fresh and is never polluted by the conditions of the outer world. Every spiritual tradition has its own name for this quality that cannot be described in words alone. This philosophy appears in a variety of forms:

- Saint John of the Cross found that secret place of the Most High in the dark night of his soul.
- Thomas Merton, monk and mystic, sought and found it in silence and contemplation in his hermitage.
- In Taoism, there is a life force that holds all things together and is all things.

- The Sufis talk about the Beloved, and their spiritual work includes "polishing the mirror" so that the face of the Beloved may be more clearly reflected in a person's life.
- Zen speaks of the direct encounter that cannot be limited by human words or mental concepts.
- Christianity talks about the Word, or Logos, that created all that is, and the way a human being can become a new person in Christ, who lives beyond the low carnal or ego-driven state of human consciousness.
- Hindus refer to the Atman as the vivifying life force behind all creation. You carry that sacred center within your own heart.

Entering into a sacred center of presence, light, and spirit is both a gift and a choice. You can create a container for it and train yourself in habits of inner attentiveness and awareness. This heightened clarity and sense of homecoming—this peace that passes understanding—can come unexpectedly, helping you through a crisis. Or you can cultivate this expansion of the human psyche through spiritual disciplines and grow into a more peaceful way of living gradually.

Coming Home to Ourselves

You know it when you feel it. It might be the sense of coming home to a place you've never been before, as John Denver sang in "Rocky Mountain High," celebrating his powerful response to coming home to the Rockies. You can feel at home with certain people, even if it's the first time you have met. It can be the remembrance of a familiar scent from childhood, an aroma as comforting as a loaf of bread warm from the oven, or the calming smell of polished wood and freshly laundered sheets dried in the sun. There is something that resonates deep within, and strikes a chord of harmony and peace in you.

Home should be a place of nourishment, a place where we become phys-ically, mentally, and spiritually refreshed: a sanctuary.
—Nicole Marcelis

The spirit of being home can be expressed in tangible ways in the house you live in. Color and beauty and order create an atmosphere that makes you feel at home. The texture of a towel wrapped around your wet body, the spring sun warming your face, the sound of a familiar and well-loved song, and a beloved voice speaking your name all partake of an eternal reality as well as being temporal experiences. These sensations are hints and invitations to experience an even greater reality that calls your name through the windows and lattices of time and space.

But you can be at home in the universe even when outer conditions are not comfortable, when you feel like a stranger in a strange place. God's Presence is with you wherever you go. Jesus said that the Kingdom of Heaven is within. Ralph Waldo Emerson said, "We lie in the lap of immense intelligence, which makes us receivers of its truth and organs of its activity." Stress is created by anything that closes us off from this Intelligence, and serenity is a sign that we are entering the gateway to becoming aware of and accessing that Intelligence. We can create lives that encourage and enhance this inner awareness or that close it off.

Sanctuary in a Stressful World

Visionary architect Christopher Alexander has been exploring how process, pattern, and complexity affect the way we build and how we live. He has discovered deep ties among the nature of matter, human perception of the universe, and the way we construct our buildings, cities, and communities. He believes that the same laws apply to all structures in the universe, and that every person has an intuitive understanding of these laws. You don't have to be an architect to understand what makes a home serene and what makes the modern world so stressful. There is a pattern of wholeness in the natural world, and humanity has an instinctive sense for beauty and wholeness. We can choose to value the intangibles of value and beauty and aliveness over a more utilitarian approach to life. We can create homes that are satisfying and human places that nurture the soul as well as house the body.

In his earlier work, Alexander talks about the "quality that has no name" yet has a feeling of rightness and wholeness to it. In his later works he calls it the "I," the ground of being that can be felt and seen in nature and brought forth by human hearts and imaginations. It comes from an egoless, unself-conscious state of being, as opposed to our more self-conscious and egotistical attitudes. He shows how the buildings of the twentieth century were designed to fit a faulty worldview that created monuments to an architect's ego and fed a system that served maximum profit and control, not aliveness and beauty. Modern buildings became the reflection of a set of assumptions about the very nature of life that were based on a mechanistic worldview that devalued the things that made life whole and healing and welcoming for human beings. The mechanistic utilitarian approach was just as willing to "pave paradise and put up a parking lot" as it was to create imperious glass and stone towers that dwarf the more down-to-earth values of daily life on the planet.

The places we live and work in have created stress. Human beings become replaceable parts that serve a mechanistic worldview. We see that our buildings and our cities and our living spaces reflect stress-generating values that are at odds with our own sacred humanity. We absorb these values into the way we live our lives. Our schedules leave no room for play or contemplation; such activities are considered to be wasted time. Our careers demand impossible work hours. We trade our birthright of beauty and human emotion for the mess of pottage we call modern living. It is up to us to reclaim the value and meaning of our lives, and to build lives and create homes where we are free to express the loving and creative side of our human nature; to value beauty and serenity and loving relationships.

We have the power to transform not only our homes, but also the way we approach all aspects of our lives so that we can create a more comforting, authentic, and human-friendly world. We can create homes and lives that speak to the soul, nourish the spirit, and encourage a vibrant experience of community. Creating homes that reflect our spiritual values can make life less stressful, more beautiful and meaningful. The matrix of our days would be set in a world that encourages (and believes in) deeper spiritual values as it ministers to physical needs and practical functions. Though we may not be able to change the modern world, we can create homes as sanctuaries that satisfy the soul. Making choices that give genuine pleasure is not a luxury but essential to our own inner harmony. When it comes to creating a serene home, listen to your heart, pay attention to what is most instinctive, and make choices that please you and make you feel more alive.

The Architecture of Serenity

Many of the structures and assumptions of modern life cause unconscious stress. Freeways and traffic noise, badly designed spaces, strip malls, billboards, and soulless uniformity are all something we take for granted, but they still take a toll on the spirit. By becoming aware that a better way of living might exist, we can make new choices, at least in small ways that help us feel more at home and relaxed. Simple adjustments can create a sense of place and home, even if it is simply by adding a fresh flower in a vase to the corner of a cubicle at work.

Sarah Susanka, architect and author of *The Not So Big House*, addresses the question of how to create a life that brings joy and comfort and a more human scale to our days. She starts by looking at how we express that life through our homes, but moves into philosophical and spiritual territory that brings insight into the choices we make and what we value most. Both Alexander and Susanka offer ideas that show us that another world is possible. Susanka shows that form and function should serve life goals. She shows that small changes can yield enormous results. In her inspiring book *The Not So Big Life*, she says, "We need to remodel the way we are living, but not in a way that gives us more of the same kinds of space we already have; that would simply create an even bigger life. What we need is a remodeling that allows us to experience what's already here but to experience it differently, so that it delights us rather than drives us crazy."

Even a small detail in a home can illustrate something that applies to the way we live our lives. For example, Susanka uses the principle of "a light to walk toward" as a key element in home design. She says that it also describes a conditioned response that's hardwired into our physiology. "We are in fact biologically programmed to move toward light, so it's an extremely useful tool in making any room or hallway feel more inviting. Simply place a window or a lighted painting at the far end of any walkway or vista, and its brightness attracts you like a magnet. It animates the space and makes it seem significantly more vital." She also compares this physical image of light and vitality to the experience of presence, of being in the moment and becoming unself-consciously engaged in whatever it is you are doing. She uses it as a metaphor to inspire readers to "move toward the light" by incorporating time for silence and spiritual practice every day. Such time offers a "window" into the eternal and invisible.

Alexander describes the design element of a "window place," in pattern 180 in his book *A Pattern Language*. He writes, "Everybody loves window seats, bay windows, and big windows with low sills and comfortable chairs drawn up to them. . . . A room which does not have a place like this seldom allows you to feel fully comfortable or perfectly at ease. Indeed, a room without a window place may keep you in a state of perpetual unresolved conflict and tension—slight, perhaps, but definite." He explains that the conflict between being drawn toward the light and wanting to sit down and be comfortable must be resolved by an organic design.

One solution is a natural alcove that feels protected, yet allows a view to the outside world. I have such a corner in the den of my little 1960s ranch home. It is a picture window with a view to the west, and my little love seat fits beneath it perfectly. It has a low sill that is easy to look out over. My love seat is ancient and overstuffed but just the right size for me to curl up in. I have been happily content watching sunsets wash over the hills from that window. It gives me a soul-satisfying expansive view of sky and color and horizon, yet feels cozy, comfortable, and safe.

Good design in the home also integrates the outdoor spaces. Garden designer Julie Moir Messervy, author of *The Inward Garden*, tells us that a garden can feel like an earthly paradise if you design with archetypal places in mind. Like a good interior designer, she creates garden spaces that combine our need for earthly comfort with a sense of transcendence. Archetypal places include sea, cave, harbor, promontory, island, and mountain. The harbor, like the alcove or window space, is a perfect blend of enclosure and view. She compares it to a child's view from a parent's lap, safely enclosed in a mother's arms, yet enjoying a higher view of the world. "By feeling securely enclosed, we feel as though we are the center of the world. One important way that we find our place in the world is by discovering harbors in which we can relax and feel safe."

When the shell you live in has taken on the savor of your love, when your dwelling has become a taproot, then your house is a home.
—Scott Russell Sanders

A Safe Harbor

Think about ways that you can make your home more welcoming and nurturing, and how you can set priorities that encourage a less stressful, more satisfying life. Just as the right design for a house or garden can offer a sense of feeling more alive and at home in the world, so can the decisions you make about how you want to approach daily living.

For instance, echo the idea of going toward the light in your daily schedule. Set aside some time for meditation, contemplation, and prayer. Set aside a sacred place where you can watch a sunset, light a candle, or sit by the fireside from the comfort of a cozy alcove or an enveloping easy chair. Make time to go within, into the inner light that shines no matter how dark or gloomy the outer conditions of your life might be. Imagine you can create an alcove of safety in the choices you make. The harbor protects on three sides and opens a widening view on the fourth. So make changes slowly—one-quarter new and exciting, three-quarters familiar and grounding. Take a new class, learn a new skill, have an adventure. But also make sure you balance newness with favorite rituals, routines, and comforting places that provide a sense of safety.

If you clog your life with nonessentials and crowd your days with false urgencies, you miss out on the nourishing vitality that is the Intelligence from which you come. There is something within you that is profoundly wise, whole, and complete.

Yet most of us live fragmented, overburdened lives that distract from and *disintegrate* that internal integrity, creating the conditions for our own sickness and breakdown. We must make choices for our own aliveness and wholeness, or become exiles from the core of our being, the inner homeland that draws from the deeper springs of life. In a materialistic society with the push and pull of demands and distractions, we become locked in abstract concepts of reality instead of experiencing reality itself. We pander to our egos when we need to make more room for our human hearts. We make it worse by stuffing too many activities and obligations into our schedules, too much clutter into our homes. Our outer reality tends to reflect our inner reality.

Set Aside a Sacred Alcove in Your Home

It might be a quiet nook, a room, or a favorite chair. Let it be your safe harbor, the place you return to when you need to recover your peace of mind. Settle in and allow yourself to relax into its comfort and safety. Close your eyes and breathe deeply. Sit and meditate, or offer a prayer of gratitude. When you are ready, return to the busy world again, refreshed and renewed.

Yet you have the choice to create a safe harbor, a protected yet open way of life. It is a good thing to combine the old with the new. There is great value in traditions and the tried-and-true ways that are comfortable and familiar. There is also great value in trying something new, stretching your boundaries, being open to a different viewpoint. This does not have to be an either/or proposition. It can be a both/and situation. You don't have to choose one to the exclusion of the other. Play with the balance and ratio of adventure and familiarity, earthly practicality and spiritual transcendence. Just expand your comfort zone a bit. Experiment with new ideas. Make modest changes in your priorities such as cutting back on activities that no longer serve you, and making room for priorities that nourish your soul.

Though authentic change must come from within, it can also be cultivated and encouraged by making changes in our outer conditions. Through simple, practical choices, we can create a beneficial feedback loop that inspires a more serene approach to our daily lives. We can make changes in our homes, and in our personal priorities, that make us more serene, more vital, more fully alive.

A More Serene Home

Home is the heart of the serene life. It is here where you nurture your soul and rest your body. Make your home a cozy refuge from the busy world, a place where you can relax and be yourself.

You don't need a mansion or expensive furnishings. Simple details like a comfortable chair and a good reading lamp, a few fine pictures on the wall, or a colorful bedspread and curtains make a home cozy and welcoming. All it takes is some imagination and ingenuity—and a little love—to create a living space that you want to come home to.

Outward actions like cleaning the house, making do with less, and creating beauty in your surroundings are balanced with inner choices that help you remember what is most important and meaningful to you. As you create a more serene home, you create a space that nourishes personal transformation and spiritual growth.

Simplify Your Surroundings

One particularly effective way to make your life simpler is to clear your living space of clutter, creating an atmosphere of peaceful calm instead of chaos and disorder. As you clean and clear, decide what you want to keep and where you want to keep it. Take advantage of clean lines and natural beauty. Instead of a welter of small knickknacks, consider an elegant bonsai plant or a single treasured antique artistically displayed. Timeless simplicity soothes the spirit, creating an oasis of calm in a busy life. An ordered living space seems to give you more room for creative thinking. You will breathe a sigh of relief in the pristine order and harmony you have created.

Cleaning house is like cleansing and ordering your life. You can ignore clutter, but it is still a distraction, like a squeaky wheel or dripping faucet. Conquer clutter with a mop, broom, and duster, and create an oasis of restful cleanliness and order in your home. Things run more smoothly when the house is freshly cleaned and the atmosphere is lightened by your elbow grease.

Use your housecleaning time to put your thoughts in order, too. There is something about repetitive work that allows the mind to think more clearly, and cleaning house can be symbolic of other cleansing and ordering in your life.

Live with What You Love

That ugly lamp was a mistake when you bought it, and it hasn't improved with time. The uncomfortable chair is a family heirloom, but you can never bring yourself to sit in it. Decide to clear your home of things you don't like. Start with one room in your home. Weed out the clutter and leave only those things that feel useful or beautiful to you. Then fill the rooms with things you love and are meaningful to you. You will be happier and more peaceful when you do.

Invest in good furniture. Cherish family heirlooms that you love, or enjoy the complete makeover of modern furniture. Whatever suits your taste and budget, make comfort and beauty essential to your style. Have fun exploring furniture stores and flea markets. Bring some special item home from your travels that will remind you of faraway places you enjoyed. Look for beautiful and unique things. Collect them for your home. Take pleasure in design and color. A finely crafted piece of furniture, a carefully stitched handmade quilt, an earthy woven blanket, or a set of antique dishes can bring vibrant touches to your home. Don't forget the intellectual and aesthetic pleasures of books. They give a house a soul and are there to remind you of the things you most value in life.

Cultivate an appreciation of art. It will enrich your life, expand your understanding, and feed your soul. Build your own art collection and hang original art on the walls. A fine painting can give a sense of aliveness to a room. A truly wonderful piece of art can provide a focus for meditation, for it will reveal many layers of meaning over time. Go to local galleries and support local artists. Start collecting art. While art can be an investment, the most important reason to buy a piece of art is because you love it. You will live with it and enjoy it for years. Make art an essential part of your life and your home.

A lit candle brings warmth and soft light to a room. Candles give a room "soul" and help create a special and welcoming atmosphere. Whether you want to encourage intimate talk over a candlelit table or create a welcoming place for worship and meditation, candles offer an easy-to-use instant transformation for any living space.

Just as comfortable and flattering clothing make you feel your best, so beauty and order in your home will lift your spirits.

Before you bring anything into your home, ask yourself: Is this beautiful? Is it useful? Do I love it?

Connect Indoors and Outdoors

You don't need fancy or expensive things to beautify your home and give you pleasure. Stones found in a riverbed, an elegantly curved conch shell, or a colorful bouquet of spring flowers can bring nature indoors, offering a seasonal selection of color and variety for little or no cost. Reconnecting to the rhythms of nature helps you slow down and connect to the elemental rhythms inside yourself. Paperwhite narcissi blooming on a winter windowsill offer a reminder of spring. The restful green of a houseplant makes a corner of your home more welcoming. Add a water fountain that sounds like a rippling stream for an aural atmosphere of tranquility and the sense of retreat from the urban jungle.

Arrange your furnishings so you can enjoy the views from your windows. Is there a beautiful tree in your yard that inspires you through the seasons? Do you enjoy watching the life that passes by on the street where you live? If you are blessed with a sunset view, take full advantage of it. Create a harbor of comfort to enjoy the view from inside. Make time in your busy schedule for just sitting and thinking, observing the beauty of nature and the round of the seasons.

You can also connect indoors and outdoors with planters full of herbs on deck, patio, or windowsill. They add a touch of growing green and can make a meal more delicious.

Gardens can create a lovely landscape around your home and be a revitalizing retreat from the stresses of the day. Create a garden that satisfies your soul. Whether you have extensive gardens with fruit trees and a host of flowers, fruits, and vegetables, or just a pot or two of herbs and flowers on an apartment deck, growing green things fills the soul with a simple, earthy satisfaction. As you get your hands in the good earth, pulling weeds, pruning, and ordering your garden, you can weed and sort through your problems, too. Try a little inexpensive garden therapy to bring a clearer perspective on life.

The simple pleasure of feeding the birds creates a moment of wonder in the day. Whether you have elaborate birdhouses and feeders or just sprinkle some birdseed on the lawn, you can spread a feast for birds in your backyard. Go outside and listen to the birdsong chorus. Watch the winged life that goes on despite the stock market, the bad news, and the daily cares of life. It will lift your spirit, putting earthly cares into a more heavenly perspective.

Cultivate Serenity

Open a window and get some fresh air. Put some calming music on the stereo. Enjoy a nourishing meal. When you create more harmony and order in your life, you'll find that you have more energy to focus on the things that are important to you. You'll live harmoniously in body, mind, and spirit.

The place where we live as well as the pace of life we choose offer a reflection of our deepest priorities. They are barometers that do not lie, offering clues to what is going on inside our hearts and minds. You can be stressed by overstimulation as well as by depression. Either way, you lose your natural equilibrium, you become off-center, you lose your balance. Making choices that encourage and cultivate inner serenity and facilitate a connection to the heart will bring you back to center, back to the home within that grounds you and nourishes your soul.

Come home to yourself by making your home more serene and by making choices that nurture your soul and make sense to you. Visionary architects and designers help clients create living spaces built around their values and ideals. You can design a life through conscious choices that honor the deepest, most authentic part of yourself. Trust your intuition, because it is a trustworthy guide. Ask yourself, "Does this choice make an authentic contribution to my life, or is it a distraction that makes me feel less alive, less free, and less happy?"

Activity: Take a Home Retreat

After a tough week, pamper yourself at home. You may not be able to stay at a bed-and-breakfast or relax at an expensive spa, but you can create a home retreat that will allow you time and space for rest, relaxation, and renewal—without the expense of travel or the bother of packing a suitcase. Unplug the media, turn off the electronics, and let your soul soak in the silence. Sleep in and enjoy the comfort of your own bed. Cuddle under the covers and revel in a morning without deadlines or to-do lists. Make simple meals ahead or buy food at a deli, ensuring that you have something special to eat without a lot of effort. Let your day unfold at a leisurely pace. A good book, soft music, toast, and tea by the fireside or a snooze in the sun might be elements of a happy day. Enjoy sweet communion with a loved one who makes the day even better. Do whatever delights your heart—or do nothing. Wind down in the evening with a bit of prayer and meditation to nurture spirit as well as body and soul.

Three Affirmations

- I am willing to let go of old preconceptions and explore new ways of looking at life.
- My home nourishes my soul and is a creative reflection of the inner serenity I am cultivating.

- I know that I am guided as I listen to my heart and keep an open mind.

chapter three

Serene Healing:
The Wisdom of the Body

If you bring forth what is within you,
what you bring forth will save you.
If you do not bring forth what is within you,
what you do not bring forth will destroy you.
—Jesus, Gospel of Thomas

The body lives at the intersection between the temporal and the transcendent. It has its own dimension of being and its own intelligence. Animals know this, living fully in their bodies and following their instincts. Just watch a cat stretch. Not only is the cat at ease, with a natural grace, it knows how to just be still and present in the moment in a way humans seldom allow themselves to be. This is a quality of life lived in partnership with the body that we can cultivate.

Athletes do it in sport. Disciplines like yoga and aikido bring about this union of body, mind, and spirit. Dancers and drummers learn to feel their bodies fully, from within, and that kinesthetic sense shows them how to move with joy, with grace, with ease. The potter feels the clay. The woodworker knows the wood. The farmer develops an understanding of the land to bring forth the best crop.

Our own physical body possesses a wisdom which we who inhabit the body lack.
—Henry Miller

Ralph Waldo Emerson, in his essay "The Poet," wrote, "As the traveler who has lost his way, throws his reins on his horse's neck, and trusts to the instinct of the animal to find his road, so must we do with the divine animal who carries us through this world. For if in any manner we can stimulate this instinct, new passages are opened for us into nature, the mind flows into and through things hardest and highest, and the metamorphosis is possible."

Enjoy the Bliss of Your Body

Most of us buy into our society's images of the body. Starving it with diets and punishing it with exercises to whip it into shape, we live as if our bodies were the enemy or something we need to conquer and control. But there is another way, one so instinctive that babies and children know it; something we know ourselves when we forget our judgments and just let ourselves *be*. Nonjudgmental awareness, an alert observation without comment or criticism, opens the door to another relationship to the body, one in which the body becomes the teacher and we are the students. Listening, feeling, sensing our way into the heart of the body slowly teaches that the body is sending signals to us all the time—even when our minds are contemptuous and dismissive. Ignoring what the body is trying to tell us, we become ill, or our pain and discomfort are so great we have to learn a better way to partner with this physical entity that is us. Flesh and bone, blood and sinew, the body is a master teacher for those who are willing to learn from the humility of things close to the earth. The body is teacher and the vessel where spiritual alchemy can take place.

If the body is in harmony with life, it is naturally a body of bliss. Imagine the pleasure of the senses when you come home from a walk in the crisp outdoor air: a sweet scent of roses, a symphony or jazz playing in the background, a delicious meal, the warmth of a fire, a soothing back rub, a loving embrace, a bed to cradle you after a long day.

Yes, there is pain and suffering. But look at how much sensuous bliss the body offers every single day, and how it reminds you constantly of the goodness of creation. A morning cup of coffee, the warmth of water running down your back as you shower, a brush pulled through hair, the color and softness of a cozy sweater, the smell of freshly baked bread, and the taste of a crisp apple. Even a simple morning ritual becomes a panoply of sensations when experienced with awareness and attention. Seeing, smelling, touching, hearing, tasting—all the senses—combine to offer a banquet of bliss, if we are not too tense and stressed to experience it. Entering into a more relaxed and aware relationship with your own body can make you feel more alive, more grateful for the gifts of life.

The bliss of the body is often felt and seen in the mysterious enchantment babies bring with them. Even in the most sordid and sad circumstances, their innocence truly does trail clouds of glory. We catch a glimpse of what authentic human nature really is. Being the mother of a newborn isn't all rosebuds and good feelings. It's real, it's raw, and life for new parents is often seen through a haze of sleep deprivation. Yet the baby's gentle presence awakens mysterious forces of compassion, tenderness, and love beyond the power of words to describe. A baby may be tiny and helpless, but there is no doubt that here is a whole person, a human being ready to grow and evolve, yet perfectly at home in the present moment.

I have heard that the body listens to rhythms the mind can't even hear. The wind and the sunset are like a dog whistle to the bones, but the mind is deaf to their high, clear missive.
—John Lee

There is a unique and mysterious essence of your true self that longs to express itself in the world. Moving from mental concepts into the body's intelligence can help you intuit the mystical image you were born with, the larger story you are meant to live. This practical mysticism embraces both matter and spirit, tracing the ways mind, body, soul, and spirit are interconnected, and how the wisdom of the senses can be tapped into for greater spiritual understanding and soul growth. Moving beyond mental maps of the ways you think things are supposed to be and into the here and now of the body helps you discover the mystical image you were born with and grow into the larger story you are meant to live.

When you move into a deeper understanding of your life beyond the dictates and mind-set of your culture, family, religion, and past experience, important questions arise. Whether these questions are precipitated by a crisis or by a growing dissatisfaction with the way your life is unfolding, you find yourself asking: "Who am I?" and "Why am I here?" These are questions that every human being on earth must face sooner or later. The body partners with the mind to bring all dimensions of your being into play in seeking solutions. Ask yourself:

• To whom do I give my power? To the one who would destroy or devalue my work and treat me poorly? Or am

I willing to claim my own power, authority, and creative energies?

- Do I judge my worth by the standards of the world? Or am I willing to go deeper and move into a place that transcends judgments, old stories, and my cultural conditioning?
- Am I willing to make the journey that could transform my life as I have known it? Am I willing to follow my heart and trust my intuition? Am I willing to partner with my body and deepest instincts to discover the next stage in my personal evolution?

Your body often knows the answers before your mind does. The body is a wise guide that most people ignore. You can use the body's bliss—or the absence of bliss and presence of discomfort—as an interior guidance system. Resistance, unease, distress, tension, and pain are all trying to tell you something. Are you willing to listen to the messages your body offers? Simply by training yourself to observe and be aware of the sensations and energies that constantly flow in a river of life through your body, you can tap into a physical intelligence that will help you find serenity, sanity, and intuitive insight. It is not a matter of fixing or diagnosing or planning; it is a skill of inner listening that empowers you to feel, see, and hear what you have missed before. By including your body in the dialogue of body, mind, and spirit, you bring all facets of your being into alignment. Therefore you discover more authentic answers to your questions and dilemmas.

Your mind is not sacrificed as you travel into this inner world of bodily intelligence. You gain a richer, fuller understanding that will satisfy your mind's need for information and decision making. You also gain a source of guidance that can lead you moment by moment through any crisis, change, or difficulty. All the wisdom to navigate life is within you, for you are connected to everything that exists. All the power, all the peace, all the good there is can be accessed in this moment, in the rhythm of your beating heart, the flow of your in-and-out breathing, the aliveness that pulsates in every cell of your body. Move into body time and discover a more balanced and integrated way to approach the stresses and challenges of your daily life.

In a mechanical way of looking at the world, *body, mind,* and *spirit* can be defined and separated, each in its own watertight compartment. Analogies often include machines and building blocks. But, as Ralph Waldo Emerson said in his essay "Spiritual Laws": "The simplicity of the universe is very different from the simplicity of a machine. . . . The wild fertility of nature is felt in comparing our rigid names and reputations with our fluid consciousness." In the emerging paradigm, there is no separation. Body, mind, and spirit are so intertwined that whatever you do with one affects the other, and *is* the other. Nature is a fecund source, not only of the physical life on earth, but of the consciousness that knits body, mind, and spirit into a larger whole than we yet understand or imagine. It offers a passage from a lifeless universe to a cosmos breathing with mystery and invitation.

An Essential Blend

In fact, the true unity of body, mind, and spirit is more like creating an essential oil blend than fine-tuning an automobile. I love aromatherapy; creating therapeutic essential-oil blends is exciting. I take deep pleasure in starting with a good carrier oil and creating an uplifting floral or invigorating mountain blend to wear as perfume during the day. Jasmine, rose, and neroli oil make me feel more feminine. Spruce, pine, and spearmint create a blend that brings high mountain meadows home to me. Each essential oil has its own signature scent and therapeutic value. Blended together in an unscented lotion or carrier oil, each mixture offers an amplified and transmuted aroma—a greater therapeutic and emotional value than one single essential oil.

Imagine the perfect blend for the essential human being: a superior carrier oil (Infinite Intelligence), then three different essential oils added to the carrier oil (body, mind, and spirit). Add in other drops of essential oils such as experiences, attitudes, thoughts, habits, choices, and relationships. Soon you have a complex and unique oil blend that brings its own particular character to life. Once a drop of essential oil is added to the carrier oil, there is no separation. Add the next drop, and the next, and all of the oils come together inseparably, creating a synergy that did not exist before.

Now imagine that you have been making your own essential blend as you create the fragrance of your own life. Every person you meet is also his own unique blend of essences, and each brings a special aroma and therapeutic gift to the world. Think of your body, mind, and spirit the next time you make soup, mix a drink, or spray on a perfume. Ask yourself what fragrance and flavor you are bringing to life. In the New Testament, Paul tells the Corinthians that they can be the smell of death or the fragrance of life to others. How can you add more life to your essential essence so that you offer the world your own unique fragrance of being a fully alive human being?

Understanding the Primitive Brain

The anxious thought, the worried feeling—where do these conditions begin? They reflect the primitive mind of the fearful reptile, scanning the horizon, alert to danger even if there is no danger to be seen. The primitive brain exists in all of us, and as we learn to understand it, we can make wiser choices when anxiety or worry would drain us of the joy in life. On some days these familiar anxious feelings arise like ghosts out of our distant past, haunting the day and dimming the colors of life into shades of black and white and gray. We create our own portrait of depression and fear, shadowing our vision with drab opinions and even darker judgments. We become frustrated trying to predict and control what cannot be predicted, controlled, or explained. Anxiety, worry, fear, and dire predictions of horrific scenarios are our reptile brain gone wild. It is the ancient mind arising, taking over today with worries about the future, regrets about the past, and a two-color, two-dimensional view of a multidimensional rainbow reality.

What does the moment say? What dimensions and depths are being missed because the mind is running ahead of the body? What joys and pleasures are lost because we are tense and on guard—even if we don't know what we are tense and on guard for? The body, in this case, is wiser than the reptilian mind, for the body lives in the forever here, the eternal now. While the mind is caught up in memory or anticipation, the body is grounded in what exists in this moment. The mind races ahead, scatters its energies, cannot focus. It lives in perpetual anxiety and stress if left to its ancient reptile devices. The body moves at its own slower, timeless pace. It breathes in the breath of now. The mind does not have to breathe. It flies back into the past, then leaps into the future; it moves in an instant, unstable and unpredictable, with a natural penchant for looking at life as a dangerous place full of predators. The mind wants answers, believes that if it could just get all the facts in order and the information properly computed, then everything would fit together in linear fashion. There is a part of us wanting to be assured that the correct hypothesis, the socially acceptable story, and the correct answer will provide the formula for the perfect life. It has a stressful, fast-paced, multitasking existence. To the mind, time is linear, moving in one direction—toward the future (and not necessarily a good future at that).

The body is wiser than the restless quicksilver mind. It feels a deeper rhythm, tunes into harmonies unheard and dimensions unseen by the human mind. The body is connected to earth time, the now moment of what is. It stands deep in the muck and the mire and the mystery. The body knows the way a hunter knows when following game, the way a bee knows which flower holds the pollen. The prey is unpredictable, moving and changing, adapting to the forest as it moves through the tangled brush. The logical mind has only the eye to see, but the body feels with all its senses. The mind focuses on a target with arrow precision, but is lost when the thickets of ambiguity interfere with that clear vision. The body just puts out more feelers, testing the scent on the wind, alert for sounds and clues, moving from one vantage point to another with its own sense of grace and balance. It feels for the next step. It taps into ancient instincts, is aware of a larger context, and surrenders itself completely to the moment. It knows God intimately as the here and now Source. All its active senses become intuitive radar to navigate the twisting and turning passages through time and space. The prey is felt before it is seen, and the hunter's wisdom is an instinct that responds to the world in its entirety.

Stretch Like a Cat

Imagine a cat curled up in a ball, sleeping in the sun. Now watch that cat awaken, yawn, and stretch out with long, long legs and torso. Cats know the wisdom of stretching. Stretching is good for the human being, too. A good yawn and a big stretch offer a simple way to relax tension when you've been hunched over a computer or concentrating on a problem for a long time. Feel the stretch, breathe into it, release tension. Slow

*your breathing to calm yourself. Exhale with a sigh of relief
and bliss.*

Anxiety arises in the intersection between the now of body
time and the future of mental anticipation. The mind wants
answers, while the body wants to listen. The mind creates stress
and resistance, while the body uses its sense radar, picks up
the tension, and amplifies it. The mind always feels that past
or future is where the real action is. But the body knows that
this moment is the only reality, the only place where choice is
possible, where life is experienced. Creating the future begins
in this moment. When we are feeling anxious, it is time to look
at what we have been thinking and choose to release those
restless thoughts, then partner with the body to ground our-
selves in the goodness of this moment. The body will give the
mind information that would otherwise be missed. The mind
will sense this grounded wisdom and set a calmer intention,
softening the focus to take full advantage of the intuitive signals
the body is sending. Our body—that beautiful and strange crea-
ture—is our home and our patient, long-suffering guide as we
navigate the journey of life. When we trust this physical being,
we are led safely home.

Authentic control comes from ease and allowing. When we
pay attention to how we move or stand, we see how our ten-
sions are counterproductive to our innate ease and grace. Resis-
tance creates pain. Our bodies—and our lives—are more easily
moved and guided into grace when we become aware of our
own tendency to react to situations rigidly. Many of our prob-
lems with age are because we move incorrectly and the body
compensates with aches, pains, and physical problems. Listen-
ing to our bodies, relaxing our resistance, being open to a new
way of understanding how body, mind, and spirit interrelate can
help us become more flexible and alive. Simply by learning to

observe and honor the body and our own experience, some-thing within guides us to the wisdom we need, and connects us to the resources and people who will help us become more conscious of what we are choosing. The mind cannot figure out the "how," but the body leads us surely to the desired goal. The body connects us to the stream of life if we are willing to be present to our own human nature speaking in and through our bodies. Connecting to body time connects us to the eternal now—high season, perfect timing, Divine right action.

Emerson said it like this: "There is a soul at the centre of nature, and over the will of every man, so that none of us can wrong the universe. It has so infused its strong enchantment into nature, that we prosper when we accept its advice, and when we struggle to wound its creatures, our hands are glued to our sides, or they beat our own breasts. The whole course of things goes to teach us faith. We need only obey. There is guidance for each of us, and by lowly listening we shall hear the right word."

I connect to body time in many ways: dancing, drumming, belly dancing, practicing yoga, using aromatherapy, walking in the woods and by the lake, planting herbs, creating art, cooking, listening to music, meditating, making collages, taking photos of flowers, and spending time just being as a I watch a sunset. I unconsciously and naturally slow down and savor my food, as I have done since childhood. A friend once told me, "I love the way you eat soup. I have never seen anyone enjoy their food as much as you do."

A personal tea ceremony with time to savor a cup of fine jasmine tea is an enchanting way to be still and know, savor-ing the moment. The British have their teatime, and even that intrepid superspy James Bond preferred a cup of the finest Yin Hao jasmine tea. On *Star Trek: The Next Generation*, Captain Picard tells the food replicator to produce "Earl Grey tea, hot."

Connecting with Ceremonies

Ceremony is another important way to enter body time. I have attended women's circles for years, where we drum and sing and pass the talking stick around the fire circle. We have held sweat lodges under a full moon and enjoyed weekend retreats that took us out of our daily lives and into another world of spiritual encounter.

In a time-out on the trail, I found an owl feather that reminded me of wisdom, a wing-shaped shell that spoke of transformation, and a red rock that told me how hard my anger felt in my belly. I lit a candle as I journaled, a symbol of the steady flame of joy that burns brightly.

My dear friend Sarah, whom we all know as Butterfly, offers a Medicine Wheel four times a year at each solstice and equinox. Her Medicine Wheel is based on Native American ceremonies but has its own idiosyncratic way of proceeding. Butterfly is part Cherokee, and her home is on the Trail of Tears. She offers a ceremony that welcomes all people. She is also a part of a women's group that holds similar gatherings, adapting the ceremonial forms of ancient peoples for modern women. I have found spiritual nourishment and sacred friendship in these circles. We call in the directions, offer prayers, sing songs, tell our stories, and celebrate the changing seasons of our lives. I carry those ceremonies with me, always reminded that Spirit is faithful through all the changing seasons of my life. It is powerful medicine to enter into body time.

Savoring Every Breath

In order to connect to the body's wisdom, you must observe the way you are breathing. When experiencing stress, the rhythm of the breath stops in gasps, and shallow breathing occurs as the anxiety of the mind increases. The body automatically picks up the rushing, running fight-or-flight of our anxious thoughts, creating a feedback loop that makes the mind run even faster. It winds the body into a tight, tense coiled spring of tension and resistance. Notice your tendency to feel overwhelmed and overloaded. You begin to "globalize" and "eternalize" everything. You think life is completely out of control (globalizing the problem) and that it will always be that way (eternalizing the situation). In reality, you are moving out of the moment and into the past, and the future, coloring it with fear, worry, and negativity. Short, shallow breathing mirrors these thoughts. Conversely, the breath can be consciously slowed and deepened, lengthening and stretching and relaxing into a calmer, more deliberate rhythm.

Are you plagued by worried thoughts about having enough money or time or energy? Observe your breathing and see if you are cutting off the supply of air with contracted breathing habits. Take deep expansive breaths to bring more air into your lungs. Let your body soothe your anxiety and remind you that unlimited supply is available for you with every breath. A deep inhalation is a powerful reminder that supply is everywhere and always available. Anxious, clutching, quick breaths tell you that fear has crept in and tightened its grip.

Soak in the Tub

When your nerves are frazzled and you're tired from a hectic day, a soothing soak in the tub can give you a mini spa vacation. A hot bath with essential oils or Epsom salts can ease sore muscles. Take a long, hot soak and let your mind wander. A warm bath with soft scents can help you get to sleep more easily. Breathe in the steam and scent. Whether you enjoy a sudsy bubble bath or an invigorating herbal soak, let taking a bath be a time of release and renewal.

When this occurs, stretch, open your arms, and inhale an expansive breath of life. The body will respond with relief. *Breathing in,* I know I am breathing in. *Breathing out,* I know I am breathing out. As the mind enters more fully into the now that the body always inhabits, it discovers rest and relief. False urgencies are transmuted into clarity and peace.

When anxiety arises, breathe deeply and consciously. Bring your attention back to the now. Recognize your feelings and release them. Move out of your head and down into your heart and lungs. Ground yourself by sensing the life energy in your arms and legs. Trust the process and observe your energy lighten up as you move from tightness to an easier, more relaxed state.

Activity: Trust Your Instincts

Follow your natural instincts and let them lead you into the wild places of freedom and fresh perspective. Take a walk in nature, but instead of planning an itinerary, follow in the foot-steps of Henry David Thoreau, who let his instinct decide what direction to take. Let your body lead you to where it wants to go. Just wander and ramble, letting your fancy take you where it will. Leave your watch and maps at home. Let your inner nature be your guide. Now take the lessons you learned on this walk back home with you and apply them to your every-day life. When you are stuck and can't think of a way to solve a problem, stop thinking and listen to your body. Be still and know the wisdom of the body, relax into not knowing. Ground and center yourself. Then see what arises. Scientists talk about the three Bs: bed, bath, and bus. When they are wrestling with a seemingly unsolvable problem, they often find that the solution or the next step in the process reveals itself spontaneously when they stop trying so hard, take a break, and move back into the body. Experiment and see what happens when you let your body be your teacher.

Three Affirmations

- I am filled with vitality, health, and energy.
- I listen to the wisdom of my body and my intuition.
- I live, move, and have my being in love.

chapter four

Serene Spirit: Meditation and Mindfulness

Read not the Times, read the Eternities.
—Henry David Thoreau

Learn to fall in love with the moment, and you will love life in a deeper way. Falling in love is an intense "now" experience. We long for the rush and inspiration and discovery represented by a new adventure in life—whether it is the sensory overload of traveling to exotic places or the romance that offers the breathless wonder of exploring a person who takes you to new levels of exhilaration and intimacy. What if this expansive awareness, this tingling aliveness, is not reserved exclusively for the highs of romance, travel, or any other high that we latch onto to feel more alive? These experiences make us aware that there is more to life than the mundaneness of our daily routines. But it doesn't take a rush of adrenaline or the excitement of a new experience to sense the bliss of being alive. It is available in all moments, all seasons, including the commonplace moments we take for granted.

Practicing Mindfulness

Becoming mindful, keeping your consciousness alive to the present reality—here and now—offers another way to fall in love, to sense the hidden dimensions and aliveness of the present moment. Thich Nhat Hanh says that mindfulness is "the miracle which can call back in a flash our dispersed mind and restore it to wholeness so that we can live each minute of life." Mindfulness is a practice that helps you keep your attention focused. Being mindful is having a calm heart, being alert and able to handle each situation as it comes. Cultivating mindful awareness teaches you that every moment is worthwhile, no matter what your experience is. It grounds you during the high times, helping you appreciate the good more fully. It sustains you in difficult times, when depression or disappointment or difficulties weigh you down and make life feel more like a burden than a blessing. It is a practice that will teach you to sense the love that underlies all of life, in all seasons and weather.

Practice Mindfulness

Practicing mindfulness is a simple way to bring your attention back to the moment and to reconnect to body time. For example, when you wash dishes, concentrate your attention on the act of washing dishes. Feel the silkiness of the warm water. Take pleasure in the clean dishes. As you focus on this single activity, be fully present, open, and aware. Set aside worries, plans, regrets—and pay attention to what you are doing right now.

Loving *what is* means being aware of the particular, how it manifests here and now. When you are rushing through life, you see in generalities, not particulars. You mistake the map for the territory. Interact with a human being and as you get to know the particularities of that person, you move from an abstract definition and category—male, good looking, single, available—to the concrete particulars that do not define but open you to the uniqueness of this individual—David, fortyish, musician, likes golden retrievers, fixes houses, has a ten-year-old son, an ex-wife who lives in Alabama, likes strong coffee and dark beer, working on his first CD, moved to town fifteen years ago, is sensitive but not ticklish, and wants to find a relationship but is still a bit gun-shy from the last go-round.

Or here's another instance of the abstract versus the particular: Remember the companies that wanted to cut old-growth forests, and headlines of tree huggers camping up in the branches of the most ancient trees so that the loggers couldn't cut them down? The loggers knew the forest in one way (and loggers do love the forest and the logging life), with much of their attention on board feet (the measurement of saleable wood), profit, and loss. The tree sitters might have come in with their own abstract theories about the forest, but they came to know the one individual tree in a more intimate way after living up in that tree for weeks on end. And the spotted owl, whose presence became the legal loophole to save the forest, would know those ancient trees in a more wild and mysterious way than any human could comprehend.

Time for Mindfulness

When we rush through life, time becomes abstract and mechanical, ruled by the clock as diagram and system of coordinates. It's shorthand for plotting our lives on a productivity chart.

The English language has only one word for time, but the ancient Greeks had two. *Chronos* can be plotted on a mental map, measured and defined. "Time is money" we say, and we cut time off from the totality of reality into separate compartments of an hour, a day, a week, a month. But there is another word for time in the Greek: *Kairos*—which refers to season, opportunity, high time. It cannot be trapped within the coordinates of a clock. *Chronos* conveys time literally: It's the fifteenth day in September. *Kairos* interprets a sensation: It's a day that the summer heat has finally been broken, and the blessed northern breeze is blowing across the lake. *Chronos* is three o'clock in the afternoon. *Kairos* is the moment I take a walk on a sunny afternoon after the first autumn cool front has moved through, reveling in the freedom from heat, humidity, and the cave-like existence of air conditioning. *Chronos* asks, "What time is it?" *Kairos* asks, "What is time for?" Through meditation, mindfulness, and prayer you move out of the abstract into the real. You move from *Chronos* into *Kairos*. You move from measurement into meaning.

Light a Candle

It's a simple little ritual, but it can be incredibly meaningful. Light a special candle and let its glow comfort you. Lighting a candle can help you set aside sacred time in your day. The candle is a reminder that this time is different from the rest of your day. It is a time set apart for you to meditate, pray, or just be present in the moment. As long as the candle burns, you are in a sacred space and a sacred time.

You attune yourself to eternal harmonies and play the music instead of looking at black and white notes on a page. Like a violinist in an orchestra who tunes her instrument to A to play in the same key as all the other instruments, you prepare to play along with life instead of struggling against it, trying to control it, or measuring and comparing some abstract sense of accomplishment to it. Instead of chaos, dissonance, and cacophony, you come in tune with the key of life. You use your whole body to join in with the orchestra, to play in tempo and in harmony and create beautiful music effortlessly. You don't play the symphony to get to the final crescendo; you play to enjoy the entire musical piece, to be in the moment, to share that moment of music with the other members of the orchestra and with an audience. You create music that is in perfect time, and allegro is not better than andante, but both have their place in each movement of the symphonic composition.

So it is in life. You no longer feel you have to struggle against what is, demanding that the world conform to your ideas of what it should be. Instead you learn to flow with what is right now and what could be tomorrow. From this point of departure, your current circumstance can become the turning point between the past and the future, the turning point that comes in subtle and unexpected ways.

The present is the only point of time that allows you to choose between *Chronos* and *Kairos*. Enter into *Kairos* and you are in high time, perfect time. Stay stuck in *Chronos* and you miss the possibilities, because you are limited to time measured by restricted thinking; you are too focused on what has been to create what could be—on measuring what cannot be measured. If you live by abstract concepts and definitions, you'll miss the life that is in front of you. Without the fresh reality that breaks into your limited ideas, you will make the same old choices over and over.

This moment, the eternal here and forever now, is the vortex of self-organizing power, amplifying positive and negative experiences into different possibilities. Becoming aware of your limiting definitions helps you release old habits of thoughts, opinions, and experiences—the negative-feedback loops that confine you and keep you in old patterns. Your habits of mind produce distortions and deceptions about reality. These habits of mind obscure the underlying mystery of other dimensions of reality, the truth that is larger than your experience and opinions would normally allow.

Stress comes from resistance; serenity is being in the natural flow of life. Struggling against this current moment is struggling against the entire universe. Fighting the way things are, and confining the reality of the moment to an abstract definition, creates resistance and rigidity. Such fighting is futile, because you are fighting to defend your ego instead of surrendering to the harmonious unfolding of life itself. Accepting situations, people, circumstances, events as they occur releases resistance. Allowing and accepting free you from unnecessary pain. You have the freedom to choose, but only in this moment.

Practicing meditation and mindfulness regularly helps you become more aware of *Kairos*, the eternal moments and the underlying realities, because you are relaxing your resistance, becoming open to less limiting definitions, more expansive experiences. As you release an abstract view of the universe, such as your definition of outer conditions, you can begin to experience the truth of what lies beneath shallow perceptions of reality, beyond your mental concepts and expectations. You begin to sense the potential hidden in the moment.

For example, you can look at a tree and just think in generalities about that tree, seeing it as if it is a child's drawing of brown trunk, green leaves—just a generic tree, the "tree" you see only as an abstract idea. Or you can move beyond the representation of an abstraction into a new understanding by seeing this tree in front of you in this moment, dissolving what you "know" about trees to see the unique beauty of this particular one—its leaves in the sunlight, the knots on its trunk, the way the branches turn and reach for the sky, the sense of roots going deep into the dark earth beneath your feet. You discover that the tree becomes a focus of contemplation, a living entity that is absolutely fresh in this moment. The more you contemplate that freshness, that "treeness" of the tree, the more you will realize that something in you responds—a part of you that partakes of the eternities. Something comes alive in you that connects you to the tree and the tree to you. You are in a relationship with the tree, aware of its existence and your existence on a deeper level than the mere abstract idea you took for granted. You are sensing another dimension of life.

The Taoist sage Lao Tzu said, "Existence is beyond the power of words to define: terms may be used but none of them is absolute." When you allow your conception to die, when you stop resisting reality because you are defending your definition of reality, something new is born in that moment. The hard, bright shell of the seed opens to let real life—life that has always been in the kernel of the seed—emerge.

During this moment of nature's emergence, the measuring *Chronos* mind transforms into the limitless *Kairos* spirit. When this happens, creative insight catches us unaware, shocking us with the delight of unexpected truth and essence shining through the ordinary and familiar, allowing us to see that every moment, every being, every situation is extraordinary, one of a kind, always new and fresh, a gift from God to be appreciated and accepted with gratitude.

Accepting Your Newfound Awareness

Within this kind of insight, the very essence of reality, all that is and was and will be, is allowed to emerge, opening us to possibilities unseen, unheard, unappreciated when we were locked in the way we thought things were. We have created space for God to walk into the room; we have split the atom and a powerful energy has been released. It does not take mystical visions and out-of-body experiences to touch this reality beneath the world we know. It is always there, waiting in the ordinary moments if you have the eyes to see and the ears to hear. It will speak to you, unveiling the magnificent potential hidden in the heart of time and space, and hidden in the heart of your whole being. You are in touch with dimensions deeper than you ever knew existed. Thus, every condition, every thing, and every person you encounter all become more "real" than ever before, just with this awakened observation and acceptance.

Accepting awareness and nonresistance awakens slumbering powers that you miss when you are caught in the trance of abstraction and resistance. Everything in the universe has led up to this moment. You are part of the whole. Your acceptance or rejection of this moment is your acceptance or rejection of the whole. Acceptance becomes the flap of a butterfly wing that can create a vortex of cause and effect to spin into chaos, creating a storm on the other side of the planet. It is a subtle influence but a "real" potential for transformation waiting to be unleashed.

No matter your situation in this moment—whether it be pain or pleasure—you can choose to harmonize with the underlying deep essence of life itself, or you can continue to fight what is and lock yourself into your limited perception. Your habitual mind will want to stay in a trance of old thoughts and comfortable definitions. It is easy to dismiss the subtle influence of this new awareness because very few people are willing to do the work to change their awareness. Yet if you are willing to walk the "narrow way" that leads to life, a world of possibilities awaits. There is a greater reality waiting for you, an adventure to discover subtle essences and potentialities that will reward your willingness to explore. Trade your maps and charts for the actual territory. You will be amazed by what a simple moment of awareness will offer, and what an open mind will reveal.

Transformation comes moment by moment, and you can never predict what a moment will become. It is always your experience, something that cannot be contained in human explanations but only known in your heart, your soul, and your body. It is simple, subtle, and without need for fanfare or Hollywood special effects. As you develop sensitivity and an awareness of subtle realities by training yourself to live fully in the moment, you'll discover new frontiers of growth and possibility.

No words can describe this understanding, but when you recognize it, you will realize that you have always known this to be true; you knew it as a child gazing up at the stars with wonder. You find it in the heart of a rose, its petals unfolding like galaxies whirling through time and space. You see it in the eyes of a beloved, in the birth of a child, in appreciation of an artist's creation. You have felt it in the purr of a kitten, the playful puppy's enthusiasm, and a laughing child's unself-conscious joy. You hear it in symphonies and in the sigh of the wind in the trees. You smell it when the rain has washed the world clean, and taste it in the sweet, savory flavors of life. By accepting the moment and becoming aware of its essence, you turn on the radar that navigates its way to the hidden heart of everything that is.

Accept that this moment is as it should be, because the whole universe is as it is. Recognize that you can choose the way you are in this moment—open to harmony and flow, or resistant and unable to change. Locked in *Chronos* or expansive in *Kairos*. Meditation is a practice that helps you release all preconceived notions and opinions, freeing you from your armor of fear, anger, and judgment. Mindfulness in the moment is your training in awareness and your point of creative power for transformation. Things may not be as you wish they could be, but they are more than you imagine.

Practicing Meditation

Meditation practice helps move you into stillness. Stillness is about being fully in the moment, in total harmony with yourself and with the world around you. A simple and ongoing commitment to meditate for fifteen to twenty minutes a day— or even five or ten when pressed for time—can be a gentle tool for transformation. Expand your meditation time to an hour and you will go even deeper into serenity and aliveness. As you learn to still your mind and body, you ease yourself out of time-bound restrictions and reactions into the peace and beauty of the eternal here and forever now.

Meditation has nothing to do with quiet reverie or passive stillness, but with attentive wakefulness. We awaken to our nearness to God. We realize that the power of creation, the energy of creation, flows in our hearts.
—John Main

Regular meditation practice trains your mind through breathing exercises and bodily postures. The more meditation you do, the more your body memorizes the feeling of peace and stillness, and the more your mind responds to and benefits from it. You become more aware of your tension and stress. As you learn to observe your own reactions, you begin to realize that you always have a choice in every situation. You may not be able to change the outward situation, but you can choose how you will react to it. Practicing stillness gives you a quiet center from which to observe outward activity.

Indian sage Jiddu Krishnamurti describes the process: "Have you ever sat very silently, not with your attention fixed on anything, not making an effort to concentrate, but with the mind very quiet, really still? . . . If you can listen in this way, listen with ease, without strain, you will find an extraordinary change taking place within you, a change which comes without your volition, without your asking; and in that change there is great beauty and depth of insight."

There are many avenues for learning how to move into stillness. Yoga, aikido, and tai chi offer movement meditation. Sitting meditation offers another avenue for practice. You can find a method that is suitable for your temperament and circumstances, from simply taking regular walks to studying formal sitting meditation with a teacher. Set your intention to make meditation a part of your life and you will be guided to the practice that works for you. Resources are listed at the end of this book to help you begin your explorations.

We are energetic beings. We can make choices about what we do with the energies available to us. Practicing stillness allows energy to flow without blocks, tension, or restriction. The energy of the life force is always available, and practice helps you move beyond the inner conflicts that restrict the flow of energy through you. Breathing and physical postures teach your body to become a clearer conduit for the energy. Meditation teaches you how to still the chatter of "monkey mind" (those thoughts that distract and demand with constant inner noise) and become an open channel for this abundant life force.

Breathing in I calm my body.
Breathing out, I smile.
Dwelling in the present moment
I know this is the only moment.
—Thich Nhat Hanh

Stillness is the power of being totally here and now, in the moment, with your entire being. You carry this stillness within your heart. When you are not wholeheartedly in the moment, you tend to be distracted, wanting to be in more than one place at a time. Stillness comes when you give undivided attention to *what is*, allowing you to experience an exquisite deep peace that helps you relax inside and move into harmony with your heart. Learning to enter the silence is a skill that can be learned and practiced. Patience and commitment are necessary. The skills are developed over time, but the rewards are worth the discipline.

Becoming still allows you to experience the life force moving through you and to tap into the essence of your own being. When you are in a place of stillness, everything becomes clear, and you gain a more detached and higher perspective of whatever situation you are experiencing in that moment. As muddy water in a glass settles and clears with patient waiting, so your mind and emotions can settle and clarify when you choose to practice inner stillness. Choosing to focus on the moment with quiet awareness, you are more able to respond appropriately and make fully conscious choices instead of allowing yourself to be driven by unconscious forces. Practicing stillness prepares you to pay attention and observe your own life.

Try this exercise to get a sense of stillness in the moment. Concentrate on a flower, a sunset, or an ordinary natural object like a stone or a tree. Just allow your eyes to notice, to be present with an unfolding rose, the colors of a changing sky, or the hard beauties of a stone held in your hand. Just be with it. No stories, no judgments. Just observe. Just be. Breathe deeply, relax into the moment. Let the flower, sunset, stone, tree speak to you about your own nature, your own situation today.

Do not judge your ability to stay still. Just set an intention and then observe. At first your mind will resist and you will be tempted to give up, to call yourself a failure. It is not your job to judge. Keep coming back to center. Be willing to stay the course and work with this as you would learn a martial art or master an instrument. Allow your experience to be what it is without expectation. You are not reaching for some ethereal high. You are merely experimenting and seeing what happens. Your skill at slowing down and stilling your mind will grow over time with discipline.

As you become clearer and quieter inside during your meditation practice, you'll become more and more able to bring that stillness and inner certainty into your daily life. Though you may be sitting in a traffic jam, you can choose to practice the stillness and serenity of a lakeside sunset within your mind. Though the day is filled with many tasks, you can find clarity and peace as you focus on one task at a time, one moment at a time. Quiet your heart in stillness and remember who you are.

Activity: Eat an Orange

Simply eating an orange can be an exercise in mindfulness through learning to focus on the moment. Take an orange in your hand. Hold its golden goodness, feel the texture of its skin, the form of its roundness. Smell the tart orangeyness of the rind as you peel it, slowly and with awareness. Take one single section of the orange, feel its soft, liquid, gelatinous texture encased in a thin membrane. Eat this one section slowly, holding it in your mouth, savoring its taste and texture. Become aware of the sensuous interconnectedness of all things. You are now connecting to all the people who brought this fruit to you: the farmer who cultivates the trees, the worker who picked the orange, the trucker who transported it to the store where you bought it, the clerk who sold it to you, and so on. Not only that, the orange you eat today connects you to history—ideas and choices made by earlier generations. Imagine the landowner who planted the first orange trees on his California farm more than a hundred years ago. Now his great-grandchildren run the farm he started, growing the same kind of orange trees and touching the lives of people today. That grandfather's life and yours now touch. As you can see, the orange nourishes you so that you may nourish other hearts, as well as your own. Give thanks for the wonder of life contained in the circle of the orange.

Three Affirmations

- I take each moment as it comes.
- Breathing in, I receive what I need. Breathing out, I release that which no longer serves me.
- I focus my attention on progress, releasing the need for perfection.

part two

Serene Relationships

Your work really begins when you release the struggle. To let go of struggle initiates a change of vibration within you. This change puts you in touch with the flow of Life Itself, which is essentially what you are. To cultivate your awareness of this flow is your real work.
—Swami Chetanananda

chapter five

Love, Honor, and Cherish:
Serenity Begins with You

If we could just be, we would be able to relax from the anxiety of becoming something we are not, getting something we don't have, and trying to shape reality according to our own desires.
—Kabir Edmund Helminski

I have worked several full-time temporary jobs in the last few years. One of my most inspiring assignments was in an academic department at a local university. It was exciting, exhausting, and, most of the time, fun. I took great pleasure in helping students and faculty. A day might include assigning an advisor to a bright and radiant young undergrad, setting up a conference room and paperwork for a grad student presentation, attending a staff meeting, working with student records, and learning a new computer program to facilitate university applications. I might talk with a faculty member about a student issue, have a serious meeting with my supervisor, or just educate myself on the ways of the academic world. Then there were all those e-mails and phone calls. It was busy all the time, with so much to learn. I would go home a bit high on the energy of the day. Still, after an evening of e-mails and catching up on my personal life, early to bed was the only way to get enough rest to face the next day. By the end of the week, no matter how much I enjoyed the job or how early I went to bed (not always early enough, that's for sure!), I was exhausted.

Create a Sabbath Time

The routine offered an opportunity for me to make a simple but life-changing decision. I decided to take Saturdays as a Sabbath. I would not look at e-mails, answer the phone, or do anything I didn't want to do. I would sleep in, and if I needed to stay in bed all day, that's what I would do. I love reading and was exploring the writings of Ralph Waldo Emerson at the time. After one particularly quiet Saturday indulging in the bliss of reading, I joked with friends that Ralph was really good in bed.

The entire day was spent responsibility-free. Grocery shopping and errands were saved for after work or church. I might take a walk, have some quiet fun (and maybe do a bit of laundry, since that could practically take care of itself), or just daydream and stare out the window. I spent most of the time alone, even though I love my friends. After being with people all week, I needed the nurturing silence of solitude. And by the end of my Sabbath day, I felt my spirits rise again so that when Monday came around, I was ready to bring my best energies back to my day job and to the people I served.

As a single woman with no family obligations, this luxury was possible. I realize that many people may not have that same ability to set aside an entire Sabbath day, but I have also come to realize that we often think we are more indispensable than we really are. Often we feel guilty about spending too much time on our own needs and interests when there is no reason but our own excuses not to. An entire day of rest can often feel like a mad extravagance or hedonistic indulgence.

Even though I have lived for many years as a single free-lancer with the ability to choose how I use my time, I have often lived as if my time were not my own, feeling a vague sense of guilt if I wasn't accomplishing something or being "useful." Yet I found that this sweet, sacred Sabbath day was rich in *being* instead of *doing,* free of guilt because I had fulfilled my clearly defined day-job tasks and hours. I also found I was more pro-ductive in my workweek if I took the time off. There is a good reason to set aside a day of rest, even if you don't feel the ancient biblical imperative to observe the Sabbath in this modern day and age. Yet even a secular quiet day nourishes body and soul in a way that no other practice can offer.

Give Yourself a Bouquet

There are all kinds of sensible choices you can make to take care of yourself. But there is something so delightfully enchanting about treating yourself to fresh flowers. They are not useful in a utilitarian sense, but they feed the soul's desire for beauty. Stop at a flower stand and buy a bouquet. Gather wildflowers from the side of the road and enjoy nature's bounty. Pluck a single flower from your garden and enjoy its beauty in an elegant vase.

Because I had the structure of a day job, I built on that structure to set aside a Sabbath day; something I had never done in all my years of freelance work. Day jobs are by nature sec-tioned into hours and tasks, but freelancing is more fluid, and it became easy for me to let work overflow into every corner of my life. I really felt like I had no time off, because the boundar-ies between work and down time were blurred by the freelance life. By giving myself permission to rest and setting a sacred boundary of time to do so, I was freeing myself in a way I had never before allowed. I was surprised by the liberating results and have kept some form of weekly time of rest to this day, no matter the structure of my workweek. A Sabbath is healing on many levels and a worthwhile experiment for frazzled people.

Because I took a day of rest once a week, I was better able to bring my best self to my church community on Sunday, and was much more effective during the workweek. I had greater clarity and a better perspective on life. If I had an obligation— even a pleasant one—that had to be fulfilled on Saturday, I saw the difference in my energies and never felt as rested or ready for the week. By choosing to set aside a day of rest, I was choosing to love, honor, and cherish myself.

I was also choosing to trust that God would be my Source (and Source for all people), instead of allowing guilt to drive me into an endless round of anxious and wearying tasks. The Sabbath allowed me for one day a week to be a human *being* instead of a human *doing*—running on an endless treadmill of obligation and stress. A Sabbath is like a tithe of time, acknowledging that we may do our part, but when we rest, we are saying that we trust God to run the universe, to take care of everything— including the things we wish we could do but are too finite to accomplish. There is great relief when we finally acknowledge that we are not indispensable. It is a way to say yes by saying no more.

Sometimes, as much as you want to say yes, *no* is a more appropriate response. If you're asked to stretch your time and resources beyond wise limits, you need to say no. Be wise about where you commit your energies and whom you spend your time with. Listen for inner guidance in all situations and act on it, even if you have to say no to someone you care about. Real friends will take no for an answer and still stay friends. Understand that saying no is not a rejection of others but a way to value yourself. It is not only an affirmation of the value of your existence, but it also affirms the ability of others to tap into their own inner resources. Sometimes your need to help or fix others is a form of not trusting them to be able to help themselves. Though the demands of family, especially young children, cannot be ignored, it only adds to your stress—and the distress of others—if you are so busy being a martyr that you cannot take time to rest and renew. You will be more able to give meaningful assistance if you have the energy and perspective of your best self to offer.

The simple intention to bring your best to life will set in motion the very solutions you need for finding time for important self-care and spiritual work. The pleasures and perils of parenting, the intricate dance of intimate relationships, and the ever-evolving demands of life itself can become your mindfulness practice and spiritual discipline. Set your intention to create a window of time for spiritual practice and self-nurture, then see how the universe responds with opportunities. The answer could be grandparents willing to babysit, a mutual commitment to creating a more mindful relationship, or a circle of friends who encourage each other on this path to spiritual serenity and wholeness. No matter what your current condition and challenges may be, it is your intention to grow in strength and wisdom and serenity that will bring you what you most need in your unique situation. All of life's circumstances demand fresh choices in each moment. There is that within you that knows what to do, and it is by learning to listen to and trust this inner guidance that you will find a loving equilibrium between caring for yourself and caring for others, finding time for spiritual nurture and finding time for meeting life's many obligations.

Do something you love to do by yourself. You have to take care of yourself before you can take care of others. It's not being selfish; it's working with the natural rhythms of giving and receiving. If you want to have the energy to be a positive influence in the world, you need to invest energy in cultivating yourself. Be your own best friend; a friend who is wise enough not only to recognize your own limits, but also to acknowledge the value of your needs. Set healthy boundaries and respect them. Then you will be able to meet your obligations and care for others with a rested body and a lighter heart. You will be strong enough to treat others well because you also know how to treat yourself.

Have a Good Cry

We've been told over and over that crying is a sign of unwanted weakness. We've been told wrong. Tears are a wonderful emotional release. Tears of sorrow cleanse physical as well as emotional toxins from our systems. Tears of joy allow emotion to flow through us to heal body and soul. Allow yourself to feel your emotions instead of stuffing or denying them. Tears are a natural stress release, and they help us process our emotions. Let the tears flow like cleansing rain. You'll feel better after the storm has passed.

No matter how busy you are or how many obligations you feel you must fulfill, you also need to renew and replenish body and soul. Time away from the demands of life is a vital necessity. Retreating from the busy world is an opportunity to view your life from a higher perspective. Consider going away for a day, a weekend, or even a week for a personal or communal retreat. If it's not possible to get away for a full day, make a date with yourself to spend one or two hours doing something you enjoy doing alone.

Give Yourself a Break

It's easy to get caught up in a fast-paced environment at work during the day and forget to take care of your own needs. If you know certain meetings or professional activities stress you out, plan a stress break. It will allow you to return to work more focused. When your day feels hectic and out of control, it's vitally important to give yourself simple time-outs for stress relief. Here are some quick and easy tips for you:

- Refresh your spirit with a brief time of prayer and meditation.
- Escape from the office for a short walk around the block or through a park, if one is nearby.
- Buy some flowers from a shop or a little snack from a street vendor.
- Drink a glass of water or fruit juice.

If you're closeted indoors for too long, your thoughts get as stuffy as the closed rooms you've been working in. It's time to get out and let the wind blow through your hair and the fresh air invigorate you. Rejoice in nature and let it remind you that life is larger and airier and freer than the enclosed world you've been immured in. Remember that life is rich and full and mysterious, and you want to be renewed in some way by experiencing nature's secrets—a squirrel scrambling through the leaves, the beauty of a leaf—even if for a fleeting moment.

The Foods You Eat

The way you eat can energize or drain you. Forget the doughnuts and coffee. The artificial stimulants of sugar and caffeine will leave you depleted. Your body needs quality fuel to run on.

Your mother was right when she told you to eat your vegetables. Raw vegetables and veggie juices can give you long-lasting energy, and fresh fruit offers a gentle boost of natural sugar right away. Nuts, whole grains, and lean meats provide balanced nutrition that will take you through the day. If you've been living on fast food and packaged snacks, try a healthier way of eating. You'll discover new energy and feel good about yourself. Snack on fresh raw vegetables and delicious fruits instead of doughnuts, chips, and cookies. Try this for a week and see how you feel.

If you're thirsty, grab a glass of water. According to nutrition experts, dehydration has negative effects on your metabolism. A decrease in water consumption contributes to fatigue. Water helps cleanse toxins from your system. Dehydration can have a profound effect on brain function and energy level. Start the morning with a glass of water. Sip water during the day to sustain energy and mental clarity.

Breathe Deeply

Explore aromatherapy. A high-quality, therapeutic essential oil has healing properties that can lift your spirits and heal your body. If you have never tried essential oils, buy a bottle of real lavender essential oil. Victorian ladies used it in their smelling salts. Its flowers have soothed people to sleep for centuries. You can enjoy a whole medicine chest of benefits in one small bottle of lavender essential oil. Called the Swiss army knife of aromatherapy, lavender is a great introduction to using essential oils for wellness. One or two drops of lavender essential oil can calm a headache or help you release the day's stress and get to sleep at night. From soothing itchy insect bites to calming frazzled nerves, lavender eases stress on many levels. Buy a bottle of high-quality lavender oil (be sure it is labeled by its botanical name: *Lavandula angustifolia*), and is marked "therapeutic grade." If possible, buy organic. And if you enjoy this taste of aromatherapy, there is a whole world of essential oils to explore. Some of my favorite must-have oils include lemon, peppermint, rosemary, spearmint, spruce, grapefruit, eucalyptus, tea tree, and bergamot. Aromatherapy is medicine for all seasons.

Sleep on It

The next time you're wrestling with a problem or a big decision, sleep on it. You'll have a clearer perspective when you're rested. Your body is telling you what your mind refuses to acknowledge. So you pump yourself up with caffeine and keep going round and round in circles over the same old territory. Listen to your body. It's time to take a break and get some rest. Take a catnap and see how it can freshen your perspective. The problem will still be there in the morning. There's nothing more you can do about it tonight. If you are so stressed you are having problems sleeping, take a bath in Epsom salts, or meditate until you hit the relaxation response that allows your mind to finally let go. You'll have a better perspective when you've gotten some rest. Let the angels sing to you in your dreams and whisper wisdom for tomorrow's decisions.

Explore the Artist in You

You are born creative. You don't have to be labeled officially as creative—an artist, performer, or inventor—to express yourself in creative ways. You do it naturally, just by being you. Nurture your creativity. Pay special attention to the things that kindle your interest, and understand that a creative passion can become a wonderful and inspiring expression of the Creator who made you as you are. Think about ways you can fashion a better world with your mind and hands and heart. Be courageously creative. Have the courage to start something new, learn something new, enjoy something new.

You will have more ease and joy when you invest your energy in what you love. This heartfelt way of living is worlds apart from dry drudgery or frantic fearfulness. Inspired choices made in love move you beyond frustration. A gifted musician loves the music; an athlete, the sport; a teacher, the learning. It is not by spectacular leaps that we move more deeply into creativity, but by slow, incremental steps. Set aside regular times for nurturing your creativity. Build skills with simple daily repetition.

If something intrigues you or draws your attention, explore that interest. It may lead you to a whole new adventure. Find inventive ways to bring love, joy, and life lessons to you. Appreciate delightful surprises knowing you are guided every step of the way. Loving what you do and doing what you love will help you deal with obstacles and problems more easily. When you take inspired action, you'll live life more fully. Working on a satisfying creative project can offer clues for living well in all areas of your life. Inspiration brings energy, vitality, and aliveness.

You can express your creativity with paint, clay, music, writing, or drama. But you can also express your creativity through building a business, making your home beautiful, planting a garden, or making a delicious meal. Delight in creativity. Learn new skills. Discover new ways of doing things. Enjoy the materials of creation and express yourself with them. Spend time working on a favorite creative project. Visit an art exhibit, a museum, or a crafts store for inspiration. Encourage your own creativity by taking a class or seminar that teaches you new skills and expands your creative repertoire.

God has given each of us our "marching orders." Our purpose here on Earth is to find those orders and carry them out. Those orders acknowledge our special gifts.
—Søren Kierkegaard

Combine your creativity and inspired intention by practicing art as meditation. It isn't about the quality of the finished product as much as it is about the process of creating itself. Slosh some paint on canvas or paper. Put your fingers in a mound of clay and make a pot. Make a collage of pictures from old magazines. Doing creative work as an active form of meditation can be healing and enlightening.

Art as a form of meditation can help you express yourself, understand yourself better, and contemplate the world around you. Pull twenty images that reflect your life or interests. Create a collage with them. What does your collage tell you about yourself? Over the centuries, art has also been a vehicle for meditating on the Divine nature. Great paintings, sculptures, and mosaics have been created to praise God, as an aid to worship, and as a way of expressing a unique vision.

Daily Gratitude

Practicing gratitude as a way of life can show you the richness of the blessings in your life. Simple things like birdsong in the morning, sunlight through a window, a phone call from a friend, a kiss on the cheek—all can color your day a brighter shade of love if you are aware of them. The big things in life are important. Births, graduations, weddings, promotions, deaths, and other life-changing events mark the changing seasons of life. But it's the little things that keep you going on ordinary days. Scrambled eggs and coffee, a smile from a stranger, a job well done, a hard day survived with grace—small miracles are easily taken for granted but make up the stuff of everyday life.

Celebrate the small things in life. Celebrate what you accomplished today. Celebrate the first daffodil in spring, the last rose of summer, and the fact that you are alive and breathing. A daily gratitude journal can be a wonderful reminder of life's little blessings. Just before you go to bed every night, write down five things you are grateful for. Happiness is found in the moment. Right now is the only time you have to be happy; don't wait for happiness to come at some future date. So choose joy by creating happiness now—and by creating it for others. It takes a generous spirit and a deep trust in God to choose happiness, but a person who knows how to create happiness is a delight and joy to be around. Make every moment count. Cultivate an awareness of the splendors hidden in the ordinary moments as well as the special ones.

A happy life must be to a great extent a quiet life, for it is only in an atmosphere of quiet that true joy dare live.
—Bertrand Russell

Happy times are often fleeting and far between, and it's easy to live in anticipation of a future pleasure that comes and goes far too fast. Have you ever noticed how often your mind dwells on the past or in the future? You're in the midst of a conversation with a friend, but your mind is leaping ahead to the errands you still have to complete. You're eating a delicious lunch, yet you replay a past argument in your mind. Enjoy the moment while it is here. Savor the meal you are eating. Be fully present with your friend. Be aware that every moment is a gift and a miracle. Celebrate each moment, no matter what it brings. Doing dishes can be a celebration of soap, warm

water, and gratitude; getting a work project finished is a rea-
son to celebrate; and the smile from a person smiling across
the table at you is all the party you need right now. Make a
contract with yourself to stay focused in the moment instead
of worrying about the future or going over the past. Breathe
deeply. Look at what's around you. Be aware of the simple
wonder of here and now.

When you catch yourself complaining, exchange your com-
plaints for praise and thanksgiving. A grateful heart and a trust-
ing attitude open the door for positive change, just as opening
a window allows fresh air to circulate through a stuffy room.

Activity: Enjoy the Music of Silence

Ours is a noisy society. The six o'clock news offers a litany
of war, horror, corruption, greed, and trouble. The front page
of the newspaper details the latest scandal. The media offers a
constant flow of chatter, opinion, and advertising. Though it's
important to know what's happening in the world, you also
need time to listen to your spirit. Ration your media exposure.
Go on a media fast for a few days. Turn the TV off and let the
silence soothe you. Instead of listening to the radio as you drive,
turn the talk and music off. Shut the cell phone off, get off the
Internet. Take a break from the chatter and noise, and drink in
the sounds of blessed silence. Seek out places where you can
find healing silence. Find a quiet church or sanctuary. Walk in
the woods or experience a silent night under a starry sky. Set
aside a quiet time to simply bask in the quietude. Let go of all
the chatter and opinions and to-do lists; just be with God in the
silence. Allow the silence to fill your inner emptiness. Create
a personal mini-retreat for a morning or afternoon of silence,
prayer, and meditation.

Three Affirmations

- I honor my need for rest and renewal.
- I enter into a state of grace as I rest in the Presence of God within.
- My heart is at peace, my mind is at rest, and I love my life.

chapter six

Playful Serenity: Enjoying Life Together

An unshared life is not living. He who shares does not lessen, but greatens, his life.
—Stephen S. Wise

Social media can be both a blessing and a bane. It can be a huge time suck; one minute you are logging on, two hours later you look up from the computer screen and wonder where the time went. But connecting to friends you have not seen in years can be a gift with unexpected blessings in its hands.

One day a Facebook message arrived from the daughter of my high school church youth leader. I had wondered how he was doing, and here was a message from out of the blue, celebrating his eightieth birthday. I remember him in his late thirties and early forties. Dick Klawitter and his wife, Lois, had moved to Seattle, following the call of God. His ministry at Glendale Lutheran Church affected me powerfully, and I am forever grateful for the good he and his family brought into my life. I found wonderful friendships, rich spiritual teaching, and a whole new attitude toward life because of the youth group activities. At the time, I was a rather lonely high school junior who discovered the joys of deep and meaningful friendships from these experiences. My love of music was nourished in the Commitment, a church singing group.

I still remember with great fondness the old purple bus, named Job, which was always breaking down. Yet even waiting around for Job to be repaired (on the first day of our spring break singing tour!) only meant that there was even more time to share with these friends of heart and spirit. I discovered the delights of Bible study, the beauty of sacred worship, and a spiritual relationship with Christ. And the good influence extended beyond graduation. I traveled with the Lutheran Evangelical Movement Gospel Crusaders in the summer of 1972. I was grounded in an open and optimistic faith that was nonjudgmental. And all this was rooted in the work of a man who had a vision of service to God that took him to the Pacific Northwest.

Looking at old photos, I see the faces perhaps more clearly than I ever saw them when I was with the people I loved. I see a picture of an eager young girl who loved her friends and found great happiness in the activities and relationships of that time. I also now see what I couldn't see then: how young and beautiful we all were. It didn't matter that I wore glasses, felt fat (photos show a slender girl), and was awkwardly self-conscious and self-absorbed in many ways. What teenager isn't? The photos show that I was in embryo all the things I have always wanted to be, and so were my friends and family. I identify with the William Butler Yeats quote: "When I was young my mind was a grub, my body a butterfly; now, in my old age, my body is a grub, my mind a butterfly."

Cherish Your Loved Ones

The body changes, the mind expands, but the heart holds beloved ones most dear, with an inner image that never fades—no matter how many years have passed. If I could counsel my younger self, I would tell her to believe in herself, to not be afraid to give herself passionately to life, and to be brave about expressing her love—both for others and for the things of life that most deeply interest and move her. When you are living it, the moment feels like it will last forever, that everyone will always be the same. But life moves on, and the *Chronos* of time takes its toll. Young men and women with bright futures will live through death and divorce, failure and loss, as well as the passages of establishing careers, marrying, having children, and growing older. In the *Kairos* of memory, they are still the brave hearts I once knew, but it is so easy to take loved ones for granted while they are here with you. Though I carry my loved ones forever in my heart, I want to be more fully present—more deeply loving—in the days we are together. And this is so not only for past friendships, but most especially for current friends and family who are still with me.

The most important things in life aren't things—they are the people you love. Love is more important than any mere material thing or exalted reputation could ever be. Instead of buying extravagant things, be extravagant with your love. Cherish the people dear to your heart, and invest time and treasure in building lasting, loving relationships. Remember that people are more important than things, and only love lasts beyond the grave. A loving heart is a priceless gift in life.

It's important to balance your priorities so that loved ones don't feel neglected. Spend time with your children, partner, family, and beloved friends. Nurturing them will also feed your spirit, for these are the people who care most for you. From performing chores at home to just being with loved ones, one of the greatest gifts you'll ever give is the gift of yourself. When you look back on your life, it won't be the big promotion or the school grade average that will warm your heart. It will be memories of the times you shared with people that will be important. Enjoy them now, while they are still here. Celebrate life with the people dearest to your heart.

Social media can be a wonderful way to connect—depending on the way you use it. I use Facebook to stay in touch with friends, both from my current circles and from the past. But I use it sparingly and as a personal connection. Each form of social media has its pros and cons. Twitter might be like clever repartee standing up at a party; Facebook, catching up for a brief time; and LinkedIn, for business connections. It is easy to get caught up in surface connections and forget that the best connections are meeting with people face-to-face. Social media is constantly changing and evolving, but the heart of staying in touch never changes. Follow your heart, even if it means staying away from the social media party and spending time with a friend or loved one instead.

There are many ways to celebrate the love of those you miss. Call friends and family who are far away. Send cards, letters, and gifts. And for those who are no longer in this life, treasure the memories you hold in your heart and give thanks for the richness they have added to your life. Vow to honor their memories by loving the people who are still in your life and by living with a lighter heart. Instead of worrying about what people think, be willing to take some risks to express the love that is in your heart and the zest you have for life. Instead of allowing the press of career agenda and the stresses of life to rule your days, choose to honor that which truly lasts: the joyful bliss of loving others—loving life itself—with your whole heart.

Celebrate Friendships

Set aside time to share with those you love. One of your greatest treasures is your time. How you spend your time indicates where your priorities truly lie. If you say you love someone, but you have no time for her, then how is she to know you really care? Slow down long enough to enjoy the companionship of loved ones. Instead of packing your schedule, leave room in your calendar for serendipity to allow space and time for Divine appointments to arise. Look for opportunities to share your love with others through a friendly smile, a word of encouragement, or by offering a helping hand.

Blessed are they who have the gift of making friends, for it is one of God's best gifts. It involves many things, but above all, the power of going out of one's self, and appreciating whatever is noble and loving in another.
—Thomas Hughes

Get together with friends who make you laugh. Cultivate a happier mood by keeping a sense of perspective. Remember that most of the things you worry about today will be forgotten tomorrow. Take your troubles to God in prayer and leave them there so you can celebrate with a lighter heart. One way to stay positive even when negative things happen is to step back from stressful situations, giving yourself time to regain perspective. Another is to take good care of yourself; then you'll have energy for cheerfulness. Let prayer reconnect you to a sense of the Divine Presence so you can see that everything is a blessing—even when it's in disguise.

Be more playful, as others need the medicine of mirth and childlike joy as much as you do. Do you know how to play well? Play should be rejuvenating, allowing you to reach for

fresh new ideas. Choose leisure-time activities that give you a
sense of thrill and adventure. Take up new challenges that give
you a natural high. Do something with a joyful heart and let the
fun be its own reward.

An adventure can be as simple as seeing the latest movie,
trying a new restaurant, going to a concert, or going for a drive
down a country road to see where it leads. Some people need
adventures that demand a long-term commitment, like train-
ing for a marathon. Others find enough adventure in travel-
ing to the local mall and having a makeover. Sometimes the
most challenging adventure of all is taking one small step in the
direction of the dreams you once set aside. Only you can decide
what is adventurous for you.

Mark your calendar and make a date with someone you
love. Have dinner with your family, take your beloved on a
picnic, make a date to go walking. Meet a friend for lunch, host
a get-together to introduce friends to one another, and create
cards, gifts, and remembrances that say to dear friends, "You're
special to me." Cuddle a child, reach out to strangers, and share
love with those who might feel left out. It doesn't take much to
make a child happy. A listening heart and the treasure of your
time and attention are the most meaningful gifts.

Be positive when you are with others. Set aside your wor-
ries and gloomy thoughts. Concentrate on the abundance of
this moment, right here and now. Your thoughts and attitudes
not only affect what happens to you, they also create a warm
and glowing atmosphere around you. Your positive attitude and
smile can light up someone's life, as well as make your own life
easier and happier. When you spread your own brand of sun-
shine, some of those heartwarming beams smile back on you.
Your decision to look on the sunny side can bring lightness and
ease to daily life.

Share in Laughter

Laughter is a fountain of youth—drink from the fountain often. Laughter renews your zest for life. If you've been feeling old and tired and cranky lately, ask yourself if you've been taking things too seriously. Maybe it's time for a good, old-fashioned belly laugh. You have a quirky sense of humor, and your friend's humor is on the same wavelength. You laugh at the same jokes, roll your eyes at the same stupidities, and appreciate the same delicious ironies in the human comedy. Laughter is good medicine, and there's no better remedy than sharing a good laugh. Humor can draw people together or push them apart, so let your laughter be kind and gentle; no cruel jokes at others' expense. If a loved one trusts you in laughter, she will also trust you with tears.

Share a Day of Renewal and Relaxation

Set aside a day that combines play and personal growth. Whether it's luxuriating at a spa, hiking in the wilderness, or sharing a spiritual retreat, spending a renewal day with friends or loved ones is therapeutic fun. Make this a real time of renewal and don't allow daily obligations to intrude. Savor every moment together. Leave time for dreaming as well as doing, and quiet along with conversation. You'll return to your busy lives refreshed by your time away.

Prime the pump of laughter. Pull out old joke books and rent funny movies. Spend a few moments smiling at the antics of puppies, kittens, or anything young, awkward, and coltish. Or better yet, pull out the old photo albums and see how much (or how little) you have changed in the intervening years. Those clothes you wore in junior high may have been the ultimate in fashion trends back then, but they may look pretty foolish when viewed through the eyes of an older self. Still, no matter what crazy fashion fads adorned young bodies, the beauty and freshness of youth still moves the heart. Whether you are laughing through tears or with the sheer exuberance of life, remember that you don't stop laughing because you grow old, you grow old because you stop laughing.

Relationships expand in unexpected ways when you share lighthearted laughter and fun. You help each other discover a lighter and more optimistic attitude when the emphasis is on lighthearted fun or creative joy. When the emphasis is on fun, it motivates you to get together more often. Your time together becomes all the more refreshing; a true break from the serious business of making a living, keeping a home, and honoring your obligations. Get together for simple fun on a regular basis. Explore new territory, try new things, or just enjoy the pleasure of being together. One of the greatest gifts for me of living in Nashville is that friends get together to make music and to savor the sound of each individual's gift. Going around the song circle blends each heart in a special kind of harmony.

Share Affection

People who are openly and freely affectionate bring each other a special kind of nurturing. If you are feeling happy, share your joy with others. If you are feeling sad and lonely, seek out others who need encouragement and you'll feel better, too. Give hugs regularly, for everyone needs to know that they are lovable. Even shy people enjoy a hug when it's given with love and respect. Be sensitive. There are times for hugging and times when people need a little more space. More often than not, people appreciate a warm and loving hug. Embrace friends—and life—with welcoming arms. Be generous with your affection. Be blessed by the giving and receiving of love and trust.

Don't forget the digital camera. Taking candid photos at parties and gatherings, or when you spend time with a friend, will help you extend the celebration and remember these joyous reunions for a lifetime. Catching people at a moment of unself-conscious fun offers a simple way to remember them at their best. Create a memory book, share photos on social media, or make a collage to help you remember the precious time you were with these special people in your life. You won't regret it: Years from now those photos will reflect not only who you were way back when, but who you have become since you last saw those wonderful people. You perceive one dimension of your relationships in the moment, another dimension when the moment has passed. Since photography is so easy and ubiquitous in the digital age, take advantage of this tool for savoring the experiences of life and relationships as they evolve.

Experience the Wonders of People around You

The world contains a kaleidoscope of colors, textures, tastes, sounds, and smells. Look at the endless array of human faces and varieties of self-expression—both personally and culturally. Get any group of human beings together and you'll find lots of differences. One of the most delightful things about relationships is that each person offers you a different perspective on yourself. As you grow and evolve as a person, your relationships should also grow and evolve. Whether it's a longtime loved one or someone you just met, give each other room to grow and change.

What you think about colors your experience of life. Your ability to focus your awareness is a wonderful tool for creating positive change in your perceptions. You can choose to create more positive relationships on a thought-by-thought basis. If you focus on what you dislike, what makes you angry, and who you disagree with, you'll find that your mind will dwell on those neg-ative thoughts. You can change your focus and choose to think about what is good and true and beautiful. If you do so, your mind naturally looks for more good. Everyone is growing and evolving, so leave plenty of room for change and respect the dif-ferent stages of evolution you each might be experiencing in life.

When you spend time with others, tender feelings can get bruised in the midst of group interaction. Be aware of the emo-tional climate in the group and considerate of the feelings of others. Keep calm and be empathetic. Your consideration and tact can smooth ruffled feathers and help people get along bet-ter. If you find yourself losing perspective and taking things too personally, release your attachment to the outcome. Step away and take a time-out to regain perspective, if necessary. If a critical remark is made, let it pass. Agree to disagree and leave it at that. Choose to look at everything—even difficult people or unpleasant situations—as teachers with lessons to offer.

Be Forgiving

Other people mirror what you are inside, so if you see ugliness in another, you are seeing a portion of your own ugliness. If you forgive another, you are also forgiving yourself. If you give to another, it is a universal law that she who gives will also receive. You create more of what you focus on. Focus on the things you like about your relationship and the good things this person brings to your life. Remember past good times and the difficult times you've weathered together.

Show Appreciation

Every day, tell at least one person something you like, admire, or appreciate about her. Honor each person for her contribution, letting others know that her opinion and feelings are important. Keep your emotional radar attuned in sensitive situations. Be kind and loving, yet keep the focus on the positive. When you are feeling angry, impatient, or frustrated, ask yourself the question: "What would love choose in this situation?" Put others at ease in embarrassing situations. Let intuition tell you whether to make an empathetic remark or move tactfully on to another subject.

We are each of us angels with only one wing, and we can only fly by embracing one another.
—Luciano De Crescenzo

Praise Others

People respond to praise like flowers respond to sunshine. A good word in season can encourage the discouraged and lift up the downhearted. Most people look for something to criticize. It takes a wise person to look for something to praise. Actively look for that which is praiseworthy in others. If someone dresses with great elegance, tell her that you admire her style. When you see someone do a courageous or kind act, let her know that you appreciate what she did. Praise honest effort. Give authentic praise to people you admire. Your generous praise encourages others to continue to do good and to be true to their highest selves.

Listen Fully

Practice active listening. One of the greatest gifts you can give another human being is to really listen to what they have to say. Most people listen with only half their minds, thinking about how they'll answer the other person before she is finished speaking. Teach yourself to listen intently to others. Commit to listening fully and to hearing what is not said as well as what is said. Wait before you reply. Take a breath before responding. It will literally give the conversation breathing space. After the other person is finished speaking, repeat in your own words what you thought she said. When the conversation is finished, thank her for letting you know how she sees the world.

Be Dependable

You've experienced the letdown when someone made an easy promise, then didn't follow through. You need to take your commitments seriously if you want others to take you seriously. If you say you'll do something, make every effort to follow through. Healthy relationships thrive on commitment and dependability. Empty promises can cause stress between people. By being someone others can depend on, you create a solid foundation for long-lasting relationships.

Share Life Stories

Sharing life stories helps cement relationships and creates a deeper bond of trust and understanding. Sharing the stories of events in your life offers insight into why you feel the way you feel, how you came to this point in your life, and what you really want in the coming years. Our stories weave together the threads of our lives, reflecting a pilgrimage of faith and hope. You don't have to be a great storyteller or make a dramatic statement. Simply sharing your experiences can create a common bond of understanding.

Don't be shy about sharing your story when the opportunity arises. You have something special to offer. Others will be encouraged by your experiences. They will be blessed by what you've learned. Even your failures and shortcomings are an important part of the story. Pick a topic and share a personal story with a friend: The first time you fell in love. Your greatest loss. The most meaningful encounter you have experienced and why it is important to you. The happiest day in your life. When someone asks, be brave and share your story.

Leave Room for Your Friends to Grow

You and your friends can grow separately without having to grow apart. Love holds people with an open hand. As you offer each other the freedom to explore, you give love room to grow and expand. As you anchor each other in your prayers, trust grows even though you take different paths. If your relationship is changing, don't try to hold on and keep the relationship frozen in the past. Hold loved ones with an open hand. Then, even if they fly away, they'll still feel free to return to the person who gives them room to grow.

Honor the Milestones

Births, weddings, deaths, anniversaries, and birthdays all celebrate important milestones in life. These are the landmarks in the landscape of life; memorable moments and meaningful passages that friends and family need to celebrate together. Remember a birthday with a card and gift, share the joy of a wedding or birth, honor the sorrows and losses. Each season of life brings its own beauties and joys, its own sorrows and losses. As you commit to your own growth and evolution, celebrate the seasons of change and growth in the lives of the people you love.

Celebrate the little milestones as well. These are not "official" occasions, but small accomplishments, like losing ten pounds, learning a new skill, or achieving a cherished goal. When you acknowledge milestones, you help yourself and your friends keep the faith, reminding one another that goals can be accomplished, dreams can come true. Encourage your friends in personal growth by celebrating milestones of progress made.

Offer Heartfelt Prayer

Pray for others. Send them focused love. Visualize the good you desire for them and the good they desire for their own lives. See them bathed in the light, as if a halo or rainbow of luminosity surrounds them. Love is the easiest emotion to experience, if your heart is open and nonresistant. It takes more effort and energy to thwart the flow of love, creating unnecessary suffering and struggle. Bless those you find difficult to love, and look past outer appearances to see the spiritual reality hidden within. You know that you have hidden depths and dimensions. Remember, we are all complex beings. Sometimes we express that complexity well; sometimes we are at less than our optimal best. You can be the prophet and seer who knows the eternal light that lives in every heart, the yet to be realized potential of every human being. Bless others, send them love and light, then release them to Divine care, trusting the process of their evolution—and yours—to God.

Activity: Create a Climate of Encouragement

In a culture of comparison, we constantly grade others and ourselves on our performance. The emphasis is usually on what we did wrong, rather than what we did right. Critiques and comparisons can sometimes be helpful, but many times they are more discouraging than encouraging. Instead of critiques, emphasize sincere compliments, honest observations, and positive praise. Encourage others by noticing and complimenting them on their strengths. Be honest, but also be kind. When you can't say something good, keep your mouth shut. Encourage others to be their best by doing the best you know how to do in every situation. Focus on potential, not just performance. Lift one another up. Be specific about what you admire and why you believe in them. You can create a safe space for people to take risks and try new things. Commit to creating success together. Set goals and chart your progress. Be accountable to each other and be supportive when the going gets rough. If you refrain from criticizing others and see the possibilities in impossible situations, you create a climate of encouragement that lets a loved one know you can be trusted with their dreams and vulnerabilities.

Three Affirmations

- I am kind in my speech and actions.
- I choose to believe the best of others and focus on each person's unique beauty.
- I create a mutual encouragement society for the highest blessing of all.

chapter seven

Joyful Service:
The Beloved Community

When evil men plot, good men must plan. When evil men burn and bomb, good men must build and bind. When evil men shout ugly words of hatred, good men must commit themselves to the glories of love.
—Dr. Martin Luther King Jr.

Community offers a supportive environment, where we meet, share common resources, work to achieve common goals, and enjoy a diversity of people who enrich our lives. Rooted in the word *communion,* community is an old-fashioned concept that is being revitalized by those who are disenchanted with a lonely individualistic society and who want to celebrate the social grace of community once more.

You don't have to live in a small town or idyllic world to create community. You have the raw materials all around you. You create a community by paying attention to the grace inherent in your situation, becoming aware of those around you, and finding ways to help them connect with one another. When you are patient, supportive, encouraging, open, and kind, you become a center around which community happens. You don't have to do anything fancy; just make yourself available to love and appreciate people.

Learning from Dr. King's Beloved Community

Community can heal wounds. In these violent times, new ideals of community are constantly being explored. One of the most meaningful and practical definitions of *community* has grown out of the civil rights movement. It is an ideal built on nonviolence. Dr. Martin Luther King spoke of the Beloved Community at a victory rally after the landmark US Supreme Court decision on the desegregation of Montgomery, Alabama's buses: "The end is reconciliation; the end is redemption; the end is the creation of the Beloved Community. It is this type of spirit and this type of love that can transform opponents into friends. It is this type of understanding goodwill that will transform the deep gloom of the old age into the exuberant gladness of the new age. It is this love which will bring about miracles in the hearts of men." The King Center continues an unshakable commitment to nonviolence and Dr. King's vision of the Beloved Community. Fundamental tenets of Dr. King's philosophy of nonviolence can be found at the website for The King Center (www.thekingcenter. org/king-philosophy). Dr. King offered six guiding principles for building a Beloved Community:

- Nonviolence is a way of life for courageous people, the vital force for change and reconciliation.
- The Beloved Community is the framework for the future, where justice prevails and persons attain their full human potential.
- Attack forces of evil, not persons doing evil.

- Accept suffering without retaliation for the sake of the cause to achieve the goal.
- Avoid internal violence of the spirit as well as external physical violence.
- The universe is on the side of justice. Truth is universal. The moral arc of the universe bends toward justice.

The Beloved Community offers a global vision in which all people can share the wealth of the earth, be equal, and yet celebrate the differences. The Reverend Howard Thurman, Martin Luther King's mentor and spiritual advisor, wrote about the Beloved Community. King was also inspired by Gandhi's example of befriending adversaries and was influenced by the thoughts of philosopher-theologian Josiah Royce. Dr. King's vision of the Beloved Community deepened and expanded the idea, turning it into a realistic goal that could be achieved by a critical mass of people of goodwill around the world. Dr. King said, "Our goal is to create a beloved community, and this will require a qualitative change in our souls as well as a quantitative change in our lives."

It is a profound paradigm shift to embrace the work of creating community. It means that we find our strength by focusing on our common interests without allowing our differences to tear us apart. Balancing the value and rights of individuals with the need for communion and collaboration, community offers a healing response to the deadly violence that would tear our world apart.

We must stand together not *against* the violence; be *for* the awaking and healing of the world—the coming together with common purpose for the common good. Each individual brings his or her gift to the community, and every gift is needed. In a welcoming community, every gift is valued. It is our work to hold the light, even if we are not addressing the violence directly. But the violence is being addressed, just as the sunrise addresses the dark.

It happens that I was writing this chapter on the weekend the Boston Marathon bomber was apprehended. One of the quotes circulating on Facebook at the time was by Leonard Bernstein: "This will be our reply to violence: to make music more intensely, more beautifully, more devotedly than ever before." I take Bernstein's words to heart for my own creative contribution to the world. I pray that my work will always be a blessing to others, will help in some small way to bring a higher consciousness forth and show more light into the darkness. As a creative artist, my words, my music, and my art can be avenues for light.

And so it is for any people of faith and goodwill. Whether you are making decisions in a boardroom or wiping tear-stained faces, building a house of love or tearing down walls of prejudice, you can change the world—if you are passionate for justice and willing to give the best of your gifts in service of life. We are the light of the world, and the darkness cannot put it out. If it is always darkest before the dawn, then listen for the birdsong that awakens the dawn. The sun will rise, no matter how dark the night.

Extending Family to Community

In childhood, the circle of love revolves around the family. Children grow and soon expand the circle to include new friends. Adolescents experience a larger world than children do but tend to move in cliques, eliminating those who are different from the group. In adulthood, the circle of love grows large, yet also becomes deeper and more intimate. As you mature spiritually, expand your circle of love. Love your friends and family, but also reach out to many kinds of people. Love those who are different from you.

Love seeks one thing only: the good of the one loved. It leaves all the other secondary effects to take care of themselves.
—Thomas Merton

Extend the reach of your love to include more people. Instead of keeping only a closed circle of exclusive friends, make an open circle that welcomes the stranger and includes everyone in the circle of love. Look for ways you can include others and encourage them to join your circle of friends. Think about a time you were lonely and someone reached out to include you. How can you do the same for someone else?

Acts of Kindness

She's the waitress taking your order at the restaurant. He's the cop directing traffic. He's the janitor mopping the floor as you exit the building. Most people pass by without noticing, but you take the time to really see these people as the Divine Presence. Practice compassion for those who serve the public. If you've been a waitress or a salesclerk, you'll understand. Treat everyone with respect and give others grace even when they are ungracious to you. Send each a silent prayer of blessing. Say thank you when someone serves you. Leave a generous tip for your waiter or waitress. Be patient. Look people in the eyes and see the sacredness of their personhood. These are small ways to practice compassion.

Cultivate kindness in your thoughts and in your actions. A word of thanks, a nod of approval, a door held open for someone, a smile for a tired clerk, a simple greeting, or a hug for a friend are all small acts of kindness that grease the wheels of life.

These actions are like small prayers, the spiritual fruit of kindness. The lives you touch for good or ill will touch other lives. Like a stone tossed into a still pond, your kindness will ripple out to others. Cultivate acts of love, words of encouragement, generosity, and warmhearted caring.

Generosity comes in many forms. Most people think in terms of money when they think of generosity. But a generous heart gives in many ways. The law of giving and receiving says that when you give, you will receive in return. But you rarely receive directly, for the Spirit gives in roundabout, unexpected ways. A generous person shares time, talents, money, encouragement, and practical help naturally and easily. Real generosity gives without expecting someone to give back in return. When you give with no strings attached, you make room for God to bring the gift around in Divine timing, from expected and unexpected sources. Consider any gift you give to others as a gift given to God. Give your best. Give with joy. Give with an open heart and an open hand. Generous giving brings joy to the heart, making your world more expansive and loving. Demonstrate joyful generosity in simple ways: giving a surprise gift, leaving an extra-large tip, taking extra time to help or encourage someone, being enthusiastic and supportive.

Share Enthusiasm

The root of the word *enthusiasm* means "to be inspired by God." Enthusiasm is contagious. Your enthusiasm can inspire others and make a positive contribution to the emotional atmosphere around you. People respond to someone who genuinely loves life and is willing to show their excitement. When people tell you they achieved a personal goal, tell them you are really proud of them. Encourage others to pursue their dreams. Be supportive of those who struggle and applaud their progress and victories. Pitch in and help enthusiastically. Speak positively. Cheer others on and cheer yourself up by embracing life with enthusiasm.

Listen with Your Heart

Have you noticed how few people really bother to listen? And even fewer listen with their hearts involved. Many conversations are merely debates about which viewpoint is right or wrong— polarizing people into for or against camps with no place for compassion or caring. Create a counterculture of the heart. Listen with your heart when you hear others speak. What is their pain? What are their joys? Focus on hopes and dreams you share in common at the level of the heart.

Build Bridges

Learn the skill of building bridges instead of burning them. Instead of allowing anger or hurt feelings to separate, bridge builders are the first to reach out and the first to forgive. Instead of creating an adversarial either/or argument that emphasizes your differences, look at ways you share common ground. When anger or disagreements threaten to separate friends, remember how important this person has been in your life. Ask yourself, "Do I want to lose this relationship because of a temporary disagreement?" Be a bridge builder and you'll enjoy lasting and loving relationships. The next time you find yourself in an adversarial situation, where people are building walls of division, start building bridges of cooperation. Focus on common interests and how you can cooperate. Unclench your fist, open your hand, and hold it out to others.

All who strive for reconciliation seek to listen rather than to convince, to understand rather than to impose themselves.
—Brother Roger

Encourage Cooperation

Researchers are discovering that the pleasures of cooperation are built into our cells. Cooperation creates well-being. Then why do we spend so much time being adversarial? Fear and anger motivate us to judge and separate. Be an ambassador of love. It's in the very nature of your being.

Though healthy competition can be good, working cooperatively with others can be even more rewarding and inspiring. Instead of dividing people into losers and winners, create a win-win situation where no one loses and everyone feels that their contribution is valuable.

You can apply this to leading committees, spearheading projects, or any situation where teamwork needs to be encouraged. You'll get more done and people will feel good about making a contribution. Having an "everyone can win" attitude encourages others to give their best and feel good about participating. Even shy people who would normally hang back will participate and enjoy being part of the team.

Help Others Help Themselves

"Give a man a fish and he'll eat today. Teach a man to fish and he'll feed himself for the rest of his life." This old proverb offers wisdom for anyone who wants to serve others effectively. One of the most powerful ways you can help someone is to empower him to help himself. Instead of creating dependence on you, you help him discover his own strengths and become independent. Encourage him to

believe in his own potential for greatness. Empower others
to become all they were meant to be.

Lend a Helping Hand

Your helping hands and willing heart are needed in this world.
Be attentive to what's going on around you and see where a
helping hand might make a difference. Start with small, simple
things. Help someone carry a package. Hold the door open for
someone. Speak a cheerful word on a gloomy day. Bring a cas-
serole over to a neighbor. Volunteer for a committee. Lend an
ear to someone who needs to talk. Make service a way of life
and give freely of yourself.

When you give your time, you are offering a priceless gift.
There is no hourly wage or monetary recompense that can
measure the value of what you have to offer. Whether you teach
a youth group camping skills, answer questions at a hospital-
ity desk, or head a fundraising committee, your time and tal-
ents can make a difference in the lives of others. You'll have no
regrets when you give your best—whether it's your best effort
on a project or buying the best gift for someone you love. You
may not be able to do things perfectly or give expensive and
rare gifts, but when you give the best you have to offer, what
you give will be blessed and multiplied in wonderful ways.

Be a Blessing to Others

Make a conscious choice today that you will be a blessing to
others. As you have been blessed, so pass a blessing on to the
world around you. Offer a silent blessing, sending prayers of
blessing and healing to each person you encounter, whether
you speak to him or not. The cultivation of loving-kindness is

a popular form of meditation in Buddhism. Here is a simple variation of the traditional meditation:

> May all be safe.
> May all be happy.
> May all be healthy.
> May all live with ease.

You can personalize these words by saying, "May I be safe, may I be happy," etc. Or you can say this to or for another, "May you be safe, may you be happy," etc. Say this prayer meditation silently when you are around people. Or set aside a quiet time at home to sit and say this out loud over and over, sensing the love and compassion overflowing in your heart. Let the energies of love fill your heart as you offer this meditation for the healing of the world.

Love is a great beautifier. It makes every plain face fairer, and every fair face beautiful. When you look at others with love, you see beyond their faults and foibles straight into the heart. Let love rule in your heart and you will discover a more joyous and blessed way of being. Love creatively by seeing the greatness within each person, no matter how unlikely it seems by surface appearances. Loving others means that you want the best for them and are willing to do something to help make that happen in their lives. Loving others is another way to love God and to build the Beloved Community.

Activity: Volunteer

Doing good work together is good for building better friendships. It's a fulfilling feeling to contribute to the greater good of others. You'll always be glad you offered to give your time to serve others with love. Many hands make light work. Quilting bees and barn raisings were an important part of frontier social life, drawing the community together for work and celebration. You can do the same with friends, creating community by working together on a project or with a charitable organization. Choose a project that connects with your passion. For example, if you love animals, you might help with an animal shelter. Contributing your time and talents to a group project is a win–win situation. There's lasting joy in merging efforts, serving others and giving back with gratitude and gladness. Choose a charity or organization that you believe in and wish to support. If you want to volunteer on a regular basis, make sure you choose a level of commitment you feel comfortable with. Lifelong friendships are often forged when volunteers work together to help a good cause. When you volunteer, you not only bless others, you will be blessed by the people you work with.

Three Affirmations

- As I share my good generously, more good comes to me.
- I have plenty to share and to spare.
- I communicate clearly, compassionately, and wisely.

chapter eight

Bringing Your Best to Work:
Serenity on the Job

Success is to be measured not so much by the position that one has reached in life as by the obstacles which he has overcome while trying to succeed.
—Booker T. Washington

It's a standard joke in Nashville: "How do you get the song-writer off your porch?"

"Pay him for the pizza."

It is the creative artist's dilemma: How do you make a living while you do what you love? Whether you are making music, painting a light-filled landscape, penning poetry, sculpting a vision in stone, or finding the right words for the next chapter in your book, these creative joys have to be balanced with paying the bills and making sure your financial and family obligations are met.

There are thousands who come to Nashville to pursue their dreams of making music. I was one of them. Unless you inherited a fortune, you'll probably have to sustain your creative career with a day job. Singers sling hash and sing on the side. Writers work on construction sites or in offices, saving their best creative energy for nights and weekends while they work and wait for the big break to happen.

Creating Magic

Sometimes the magic happens. I used to go to a songwriter's night at Davis–Kidd Booksellers' Second Story Cafe (now long gone, unfortunately). Each Friday night there was a lineup of up-and-coming writers with a final set from a pro writer.

I'll never forget hearing the story of one successful song-writer-turned-pro who told about his first radio hit back in the mid-1990s. He had moved to Nashville a few years earlier in search of fame and fortune. Like most songwriters who move to town, he was supporting his music with a day job, which in his case was delivering pizzas. He drove around town in his beat-up old pickup, schlepping pizzas for tips and minimum wage. One long and discouraging day, he had delivered yet another pizza to a customer in the pouring rain. To add insult to injury, there was no tip. Tired and dripping, he got into the front seat and turned on the radio. A familiar song was playing—it was one of his songs! He didn't even know it had been released to radio, so it was a total surprise. He said that he just laid his head on the steering wheel and cried. It was his first big break and the opportunity that led to a successful career as a country song-writer. That song got him the full-time writing deal that let him focus on his music and leave his career as pizza delivery boy behind.

I have known many talented and deserving musician friends who got writing deals but no hits. And some hit makers who rode high on the charts then had their career crash, causing them to totally reinvent themselves. They have watched the winds of change blow away their dreams of making it in the music industry. They have faced the disappointments with courage, even as they struggled to find a meaningful way to make a living. One incredibly talented friend of mine lost his songwriting deal and ended up working part-time at Home Depot and giving guided tours at the local auto factory. I admire my creative friends. If a day job was necessary, I have found my friends to be faithful, working for money while pursuing their music dreams. There were some who discovered along the way that the day job was so satisfying, they made it a way of life and let their music become a part-time gig instead of chasing the full-time music career. With grace and style, my friends have taught grade-school children the joy of music, worked on remodeling old houses or building new homes, counseled in recovery centers, programmed computers, and, yes, even waited tables. They have made a positive difference through loving service wherever they landed in life. And they still stay true to their music, still love to gather around the writer's circle and share the new song they just wrote.

The Hidden Gifts of a Day Job

I have had my own share of day jobs and discouragement. For almost twenty years, I was blessed to have freelance work writing marketing materials for book publishers. It was closer to the dream than delivering pizzas but still a long way from seeing my personal writing dreams come true. I have also had additional day jobs, both in my younger years and in the years following the Great Recession of 2008. I used to rebel and complain about my jobs when I was in my twenties, making myself and all the people who had to be around me miserable. While working several day jobs over the last few years, I learned a thing or two about showing up at work without judgment and complaining, taking one moment at a time when stressed, and letting go of all my inner protests at having to scramble to make a living again.

I found the gifts hidden in the heart of the day job. My Saturday job at the art gallery gave me a safe and beautiful place to be, as well as an education in art. Working temp assignments at a university and medical center built my confidence. These day jobs introduced me to funny and fascinating people whom I would never have known if I had still been immersed in my small freelance world. I was able to pay bills again, but I was also enriched by new relationships and the perspectives made available through being a part of larger organizations that were making a positive difference in the world. I know the joy of serving with a grateful heart. Even on difficult days, the decision to quietly serve, bless those I work with, and just be present with no judgment or agenda has proven to be a satisfying and inspiring way to spend my days. I am enriched by these experiences, and, even when my fortunes change, I get to write and do what I love best; my day job experiences have made me a better writer and a better person.

Whether you are working to pay the bills or are immersed in the career of your dreams, there is always a bread-and-butter aspect to any working situation. Work is work, even work you love. So much of life is spent serving others and working collaboratively for some form of pay. So how can you make work more enjoyable and less stressful?

Bring Your Highest Self to Work

You are part of something larger than your personal story, so make a firm decision that you will bring your highest self to work. Meditation and mindfulness can help you make the transition from private life to public engagement, and help you be more effective on the job. When you bring your highest self to work, a spiritual alchemy can work in, through, and for you. The atmosphere you create at work begins within. When you bring an expansive and peaceful presence to the workday, you have the potential to transform, at least in a small way, the atmosphere at work. Recognize that you are connected at the heart to everyone—even the difficult people. This is a biological fact as well as a spiritual reality.

Your work is going to fill a large part of your life, and the only way to be truly satisfied is to do what you believe is great work. And the only way to do great work is to love what you do. If you haven't found it yet, keep looking. Don't settle. As with all matters of the heart, you'll know it when you find it.
—Steve Jobs

Find a job you love and you'll never have to "work" a day in your life. If you love to do something, it doesn't feel like work, even if you work hard doing it. As a child, you dreamed of growing up and doing something wonderful. As an adult, finding your lifework may be more complex. If you're in a job that's more work than pleasure, perhaps you need to reconnect with childhood dreams and find something closer to your heart's desire. When you love what you do, you do your work well. You put energy and passion into every task, even the repetitive and mundane work. When you have a job, but it's not what you love, choose to find ways to love, or at least like, it. You reap what you sow. Sow as much loving service and thoughtful excellence as you possibly can. Look for ways to love what you do even if you are not doing what you love. Consider it a seed of faith planted for the day when you will be doing what you love. Though you may not have a perfect job, you can take pleasure in work well done.

There is no one-size-fits-all formula for success, because we each define success differently. The secret of success is being true to your heart's deepest desires, seeking the best for yourself and others. Success may mean money, power, or prestige—or it may mean more intangible rewards. Success can be found in a talent developed, a garden tended, a child loved, and beauty created. True success is finding good work that allows you to develop your talents and serve others. Work offers a place for community and service. Work pays the bills, nurtures the family, tends the garden, keeps the home, develops the skills, and offers a place to grow in creativity and service.

Keep faith in the work itself and do it well, giving it your best effort. Work done in the right spirit can be incredibly satisfying. It is a form for the natural expression of your abilities and creativity. When you work wholeheartedly at something, you forget yourself. Completely absorbed in the task at hand, you lose track of time and plunge into the simple pleasure of accomplishing good or making the world a better place. Whether your work is making beds and doing dishes or running a business, put your heart into your work, and the work itself will be its own reward.

Set an intention to create a wholesome, healthy, and nourishing atmosphere in the workplace for yourself, your coworkers, your clients and customers. Create a harmonious work space that enhances work flow. Invest in the equipment you need to do the job. Dress for success, whatever that looks like in your field. In an office, make sure your chair is at the right height, the angle of your computer screen doesn't cause strain, and you have good lighting so you can see clearly. Focus on doing whatever task is at hand with loving attention.

If you run into challenges on the job, a simple change of attitude can make life easier. Making the best of a situation helps you cope with difficulties and make more of opportunities. If you've been wrestling with a problem, learn to view challenges as opportunities and problems as projects. Instead of defining it as a problem, with all the dead-end feelings of despair, helplessness, and frustration that are attached to the word *problem,* call it a project instead. The word *project* suggests a process that leads to a positive outcome. A project is something you can work on and learn from.

A shift in definition can inspire a shift in perspective. A project begins with a plan. So create an action plan that turns a problem into a project you can work on. Simple action steps that are easily measurable will help you keep going when the going gets tough. A good plan offers a solution to problems and keeps you focused on your purpose and goals.

Emotional Intelligence at Work

When you look at others, see them with eyes of serene clarity. Look through the lens of love and see behind the human face to behold the eternal face of glory that looks out at you from behind the masks of personality, ego, and earthly roles. See this in those who serve you, in those you serve, in those who irritate you, and in those you like and enjoy.

If you have a difficult supervisor or troublesome clients or customers, set an intention to look past the surface. Look for the good in each person, forgive the bad. Do what you can to satisfy the customer, especially in businesses that emphasize that the customer is always right. If you do your best but still cannot satisfy a challenging person, understand that it is not your problem, it is about their problem. Be diplomatic, but don't let anyone push you too far. You can be kind and caring without allowing others to step on you or treat you disrespectfully.

Learning to respect yourself can teach you to respect others' feelings, hopes, and dreams. Love your neighbor as yourself.

Respect others' right to be different and to have their own opinions and ways of doing things.

It's easy to find things to criticize in others. People make mistakes. They do foolish things. You can pick on people's weaknesses—or you can encourage their strengths. Focus on what is good in others instead of on what is wrong. Look for what is true and beautiful in each person you encounter today. Recognize the richness of experience represented by this person you are encountering. Is your not-so-favorite boss criticizing or playing politics again? Choose to focus on the fact that your boss wants to feel good, and see the worthy aspects of her personality. If your customer irritates you, take a deep breath and remember to honor and serve this unique human being well. You are touching the lives of all the people your client or customer touches. A happy person spreads happiness, an unhappy person spreads unhappiness. Instead of taking it personally, make it a loving game to see if you can't make this person's day better and bring out the best in them.

Tell others what you like or admire about them. People respond to the way you treat them. Your appreciation can help bring out the best in others. Have compassion for the struggles we share in common as human beings. Admire the beauty and excellence, forgive the foolishness, and appreciate the differences. The next time you find yourself about to say something critical about someone's weakness, exchange that thought for a sincere compliment emphasizing a strength.

It's easy to judge by surface appearances. But snap judgments lock you into one way of looking at a situation or person. It's only human to want to be right, and you'll unconsciously defend your own judgment, even if facts later reveal that you might be wrong. Leave your options open and don't make a premature decision about the rights and wrongs of a situation or person. Keep an open mind and watch for the truth hidden below the surface to be revealed.

Practice the art of forgiveness. Difficult people are often hurting people, and their unkind actions are often an unconscious repeat of the way they have been treated in the past. A demanding supervisor may criticize you, but that criticism can be an echo of the voices from her past, not about you at all. She honestly may not be conscious that her pattern of relating to others is not productive. It might have achieved results in the past, but if it does not honor and encourage others, it will grow less effective as time goes by.

Dealing with Difficult People at Work

If you deal with a difficult person or challenging situation at work, don't take things personally. And don't retaliate, justify, blame, or condemn. All of that creates resistance in your heart and mind, giving energy to the problem and trapping you in unproductive responses. Rehearsing old wrongs in your mind, holding onto grudges, and looking for the worst in someone who has hurt you is counterproductive. Righteous anger usually contains a call to action. But destructive anger goes around and around in circles, pointing the finger of blame and condemning others. Destructive anger is more concerned with being right and making others wrong.

Honor the Differences

The world contains an endless kaleidoscope of humanity. Gather any group of human beings together and you'll find lots of differences—especially in a work environment. Make it a point to honor the differences as well as the things you have in common. Enjoy the fact that others are different from you. Instead of merely arguing sides of a question, leave room in your conversation for people to share why they believe or act the way they do. Let others teach you, even when you disagree with them.

Don't let anger or self-justification rule in your heart. Your unwillingness to forgive contributes to the problem, making the situation much more difficult than it has to be. You have a choice. You can continue to withhold forgiveness, or you can choose to forgive the other person, let go, and move on. No matter what the other person chooses to do, your choice to forgive frees you from the chains of the past.

Go beyond mere forgiveness. See this difficult person as a teacher. You may not like the lesson, but the things that trigger negative feelings offer an instantaneous test of the hidden attitudes and beliefs that rule your life. A critical remark awakens the hurt child who still remembers being tormented by a grade-school bully. But this time you are not a young child but an adult who can claim a higher perspective and a different response. The criticism can be examined for validity. Does it offer information that will help you or help you do your job better? Or is it just another power play by someone who is insecure? Perhaps the critic is only echoing the negative job performance review that made her wonder if she was going to get that longed-for promotion. Her doubts might be coloring all her interactions, and work colleagues can often catch the fallout from those unspoken fears and disappointments.

Seeing this situation in the light of your inner values and priorities, the observing mind steps back from the irritation and pain to show you a larger picture. You know instinctively whether the criticism is valid or not. Trust that instinct. Trust also that if a challenging situation arises, the Universe may simply be asking, "Do you really want this? Or do you want to choose a different pattern, a better response?" There is no good reason to take someone else's abuse. But there is wisdom in weighing your response and choosing to understand the dynamics of a relationship or situation before making snap judgments. When you respond thoughtfully instead of reacting emotionally, you come from a place of personal power.

If emotions are charged, break away from the situation if at all possible. Meditate for calm and insight. Five minutes away from the office or even one minute at your desk can help you calm down and get a better perspective on what your response should be. Take a meditative walk in a park at lunch. Go within when the outer conditions are chaotic, stressful, or troubling. Listen to your intuition. Let events unfold and stay in the observer mind-set, allowing what is without judging or condemning. Trust your instincts, especially under pressure. Instead of blaming others, or even yourself, when things go wrong, choose to focus on what you can do and where you can go from here. What's done is done. Concentrate on getting something good out of a painful situation. Listen for inner guidance and realize that with the right attitude, anything can be a lesson in the school of life.

Your success and happiness lie in you. External conditions are the accidents of life. The great enduring realities are love and service.
—Helen Keller

Just because others in the workplace are focused on wrong priorities, use high-pressure tactics, or are in denial about an unpleasant or toxic atmosphere does not mean you have to live that way. You can choose to create your own microclimate of peace and serenity. Live in peace and focus on doing your work mindfully. If your work is incompatible, start taking small steps toward finding or creating other work. When you come from love instead of fear or anger, your choice will be reflected in the way others respond to you. You defuse stress by becoming more honest, more humorous by taking life just a bit more lightly, and less fearful, not only for yourself, but for those around you.

Give yourself—and others—a chance to cool off. If the situation feels too explosive or confrontational, walk away. Pray about it and wait until everyone gets some distance from the emotion of the moment. Ask yourself, "What can I do in *this* moment, here and now?" Trust that where you are now is where you are supposed to be, and trust that setting an intention and listening to the inner guidance will take you where you want to be or help you create a solution that works for the highest good of all.

Managing the Politics

Sometimes the politics and people preclude success on the job, no matter how hard you try. I have seen this in the way a supervisor will treat different employees. One is favored, offered all kinds of perks and approval. Another employee, equally hardworking and capable, is not given everything she needs to do her job, expected to flounder on her own, and runs into resentment and disapproval—no matter how positive she is or how well she handles the challenges of the job. You cannot force people to like or approve of you in situations like that. You cannot coerce someone into treating you fairly. You just have to step back and stop taking it personally. If a person at work doesn't like you (no matter how supportive she pretends to be publicly), it is her problem. Search your own heart and see if there are reasons for her dislike. Make sure you are clear and doing your best.

Delight in the Accomplishments of Others

Does your heart ever sink when you hear about another's good news or success? Have you rejoiced in your secret heart when you heard that someone whom you envied suddenly runs into trouble or failure? Envy and jealousy are subtle, selfish poisons. The best antidote to poisonous green envy is to consciously choose to rejoice in the successes and accomplishments of others. See their success as your success, for a heart that reflects loving generosity will one day reap its own reward.

Don't add to the negative energy by reciprocating with more negative energy—even in your private thoughts. One sip of the poison of judgment, criticism, or self-righteousness can send you into a binge of toxic negativity. If necessary, write your feelings in a journal, then let it go. Drop the script. Stop telling the negative story. Remember, you know only part of the truth, not the whole story. You have no idea of how grace may be working behind the scenes. Put yourself in the other person's shoes and try to understand the challenges and hurts that might be at the root of her behavior. Make it your priority to give her what you wish she could give you: kindness, fairness, and support.

For example, if you have a difficult supervisor, think about the challenges she faces. First of all, you may think you're doing a good job, but you might not necessarily be a perfect angel to work with either. Think about the demands placed on your supervisor. Does she have a demanding supervisor above her? Is there cost cutting at the company that makes getting the same results with fewer resources a constant worry? How many hats does your supervisor have to wear? Could you face the responsibilities and challenges she faces and still be patient and kind? What about the obstreperous, obnoxious employee whom everyone hates to deal with? If your supervisor is responsible for her performance and for keeping up staff morale, having to deal with the difficult employee and with disgruntled staff isn't going to make your supervisor's job any easier. Would you want that job? Now think about how easy (or difficult) dealing with you might feel to someone else. You can make it more difficult by finding fault, whining, and complaining. Or you can look for ways to be positive and supportive, even if you may not be entirely happy with your supervisor's choices. Give your supervisor the respect you would like to receive.

If you have done all you can to meet expectations and contribute your best to the work, yet it still does not change the situation between you, understand that it is not about you. Focus on the positive in the situation and on the person who pushes your buttons; the lessons may very well be about how you can move beyond prejudice and rejection. If the situation continues to be toxic, it may be time to make a graceful exit. Even if you stay on the job working with a difficult and demanding person, give yourself (and that person) emotional space. Set your own boundaries for personal safety and sanity. Be willing to walk away if necessary—no matter the cost.

Be aware when problems from the past are being projected onto people in the present. Understand that you may be a reminder of some unhappy circumstance from that individual's past. Remember that this is an opportunity to practice unconditional love and forgiveness. Be a diplomat: Walk softly and honor even your most difficult enemy. No matter what guise the opposition comes in, if you look into that person's heart, you will see that this is a Divine appointment and this person is teaching you about yourself. There would be no response within you if there was not something in this person that strikes an emotional chord. Forgive yourself. Forgive your adversary. Meditate and pray. Listen for guidance.

Each situation is unique, so only step-by-step, moment-by-moment awareness will show you how to bring healing to this challenging work relationship. In the process, you may discover that this person was not only bringing out the worst in you, she was also challenging you to take life to a higher level and become a better version of yourself.

If love is the strongest force in the world, learn how to love more deeply, transcending your own limited ways of relating to others. Learning to love, honor, and forgive a difficult colleague may not transform your working relationship, but it can transform you. Bad behavior is a cry for love, so see this person through the eyes of God. If you can do that, you will see the person she was meant to be, the friend you could have shared the work with. Bless her and honor the choices she makes—even if you don't agree with them—and know that God will resolve the issues in ways you cannot imagine.

Create a counterculture of the heart. Listen with your heart when you hear others speak. What is their pain? What are their joys? What hopes and dreams do you share? The attitudes you cultivate can have a powerful effect on others. How do you feel when you sit next to someone who is restless? You pick up some of her restlessness. Anger, fear, impatience—strong negative feelings can be contagious. But positive emotions also can be contagious. Make a conscious choice to cultivate peace and positive emotions in your heart. Resolve that with Divine help you will find reasons to rejoice rather than reasons to complain. Respond to difficult people and challenging situations with serene faith and conscious awareness. As you develop qualities of calmness and nonattachment, others will be influenced by your attitude. At the very least, you will not contribute more negative energy, and at the very best, your serene presence and positive attitude may become an avenue for unexpected opportunities to create something better and more satisfying.

Activity: Redefine Success

How do you define success? Money? Education? Good looks? Social standing? An impressive outward image? If you've been feeling as if you don't measure up, maybe you need to redefine what success means to you. Success can be found in building a solid business, doing good work, raising a healthy family, serving your community, creating a welcoming home, encouraging friends, or simply doing your best every day. There is no one-size-fits-all formula for success. You can measure your life by a different standard, one that satisfies the heart. True success is a life well lived, in harmony with Divine priorities. When it comes to the most important choices in life, it is the heart's wisdom that guides you. When it's a choice between love and logic, let love be the deciding factor. Focus on something that makes you happy to be who you are. Evaluate your present goals. Are they consistent with your innate gifts and talents? Do you see them as fulfilling a higher purpose for your life? While the world may applaud outward achievements, only you know in your heart of hearts if what you are doing honors your deepest values.

Three Affirmations

- God is my business partner, and God is always successful.
- I receive my good from many sources, and my good comes to me in expected and unexpected ways.
- I love my work and I honor my colleagues as we create greater good for the world.

part three

Serenity in the Storm

Be not the slave of your own past—plunge into the sublime seas, dive deep, and swim far, so you shall come back with self-respect, with new power, with an advanced experience that shall explain and overlook the old.

—Ralph Waldo Emerson

chapter nine

Serenity through Crisis and Change

All changes, even the most longed for, have their melancholy; for what we leave behind us is a part of ourselves; we must die to one life before we can enter another.
—Anatole France

Change comes whether we feel ready for it or not. You cannot stop change. It is as inevitable as the seasons, as unpredictable as the weather. Some changes are welcome; others, not so welcome. But even welcome change brings stress. Events that cause sudden or drastic changes in our lives are often the most stressful.

Illness, divorce, a death in the family, and unemployment are less than welcome changes that we expect will make life more stressful. But changes we consider positive, like a new marriage, a new baby, or buying a new house, also bring stress in their wake.

All change, even change that brings better and much desired circumstances, is a journey into the unknown. We are such creatures of habit that we prefer to stay safely and comfortably in our rut. We like life to be predictable. We want to think we are in control. For many years, we might be able to contain life and stay in our comfort zones. But sooner or later, change will come. Whether in cataclysmic crisis or incremental growth, change must be dealt with. The question is: will you fight change or be open to what life brings?

Tracing the Path of Change

Think about all the changes in your life over the years. Here's an exercise that offers perspective on the seasons of change. Take a few pieces of paper and chart your life in ten-year increments from the day you were born until now. Use one piece of paper for each decade. If you want to go into more detail, do five-year increments. Think about where you were and what you were doing and what your world was like. Write about it keeping these questions in mind:

- Where were you living and whom were you living with?
- What were your tasks, work, and obligations?
- What did you most enjoy doing?
- How did you feel about yourself?
- Who were your friends and colleagues?
- What dreams did you carry in your heart?
- What accomplishments gave you a feeling of pride?
- Who were your mentors and teachers?
- What kind of clothes did you wear?
- What was happening in popular culture, including politics, music, movies, clothing, slang, and technology?
- Who was most important in your life?

Think about expectations you had in each decade and what the world was like for you back then. The challenges you faced in grade school were different from the challenges of young adulthood. You grew, you learned, you encountered new experiences and met new people. Your relationships changed along with your evolving life circumstances. One decade might mean that learning to ride a bicycle or pass a history test were important challenges, another decade might bring a new job, a marriage, or the birth of a child or a grandchild. Key career changes, moves, and long-term commitments colored your world.

The older you are, the more changes you have experienced. It's reassuring to look back and see how you survived difficulties, surmounted obstacles, and enjoyed successes. You even survived dreadful fashions, cultural crazes, and bad hairdos! This exercise helps you see that as life changed, you evolved. When it seemed that nothing would ever change, that life was static, you can look back now and see that the past is like a dream, an ever-moving caravan of change. Everything changes, and the world you knew decades ago has been transformed into a different world today.

Making Change Easier

Clinging to the past is futile. Though you might crave the comforts of what you already know, it is the nature of life to grow, evolve, and change. Human beings grow through the seasons of life, moving from childhood into adolescence, and then adulthood, from immaturity to maturity.

Instead of fearing change, embrace it. Since you know change is inevitable, make changes that will improve your life. Think about your priorities and choose actions that make life easier, simpler, and happier. Whether you are getting in shape, contemplating a career change, or clearing clutter from your office, small, easy actions will add up to big changes over time. Start slowly and build gently. Life is much less complicated when you don't bite off more than you can chew.

Believe in yourself. Give yourself credit for the victories won. Give yourself grace for the losses and setbacks. Calm confidence from within reflects in your outer life. Dare to believe that you can achieve your goals, overcome your difficulties, and fulfill your unique destiny. Embrace change not only to create a better life, but also to honor those who have gone before. You may not be able to pay them back, but you can pay the love forward.

Most growth, including spiritual growth, comes gradually and often imperceptibly over time. Whether you proceed gently step-by-step or fall down and pick yourself up, keep going, stay open, continue to believe that God has work for you to do or you wouldn't be here. Let change show you a better way of being. Let the seasons of life unfold in their own natural grace. Embracing change means that you are open to fresh opportunities and new possibilities. Choose a deeper way of trust today and welcome change into your life.

Be Open to Change

How often have you clutched at the status quo, fighting the natural forces of change, trying to control and confine life within the small boundaries of your fears and expectations? Move beyond rigid opinions and limited ideas. Let go of old attitudes that no longer serve you and release old expectations and disappointments.

Losses, layoffs, deaths, sudden changes—life takes its toll, and you begin to be afraid that the road of life has turned into a dark and dangerous dead end. Unexpected detours happen. Tough times have their seasons. But the seasons change, and what you thought was the end of the road may turn out to be only a bend in the road.

Remember that every detour and delay can be an opportunity to examine your priorities and get clear on what is truly important to you. This could be a time to simplify your life, eliminating distractions that hold you back.

If you are holding onto the past, you're carrying dead weight. You cannot bring the good things of the past back, and you cannot right past wrongs by obsessing over them today. Choose instead to release the past and trust in Divine Grace for today.

Be thankful for today instead of rerunning old, sad stories in your mind. You'll find you have more energy to enjoy life now. Create a new story. Choose to embrace this day, trusting that God will bring even more good tomorrow. See abundance instead of loss, possibility instead of unmet expectations. Release the past with love and gratitude, and rejoice in this moment.

Learn from Your Mistakes

Everyone makes mistakes. But the greatest mistake you can make is to refuse to learn what they can teach you. When you are willing to learn from your mistakes, you will no longer need to define them by what went wrong but by the lessons they taught you so you could do better.

Mistakes are the construction zones of life that make you slam on the brakes and ask yourself, "What's going on here?" They are reminders that everyone, no matter how young or old, is a work in progress. Realize that you win some and you lose some. Laugh at some of your mistakes. Enjoy the process, viewing mistakes as opportunities to learn and grow instead of disasters to deny or defend.

Mistakes, loss, errors, and failures are often the fertile compost that helps you grow a better life. Concentrate on where you are going, not where you have been. Learn from your errors and move beyond them. Do you blame yourself for what cannot be changed? Never waste energy in guilt, self-justification, or regret. Instead, accept what happened and move on.

Mistakes are part of the process. Learn from them and don't be afraid of making more mistakes. Like a child who stumbles as she's learning to walk, pick yourself up and keep on walking. Lighten up, stop judging yourself, and let your mistakes be your teachers. It's all part of the learning process. When you look back, you'll realize that there were no mistakes, only interesting choices.

Sow Seeds of Faith

A tiny seed holds the potential for leaves, flowers, or fruit when it's planted in rich soil, watered, and cultivated. A simple affirmative choice holds the same creative power when you plant it in the soil of faith and tend it with love. When you have a mountain to move, start by planting a seed of faith through affirmation and action.

It doesn't have to be complicated. Set your intention, then give thanks that the answer is coming, even though you may not yet know when. Make a marker in your garden of faith, and then give it time to grow in Divine Grace. Write down an affirmation of faith. Put it on an index card and carry it in your pocket or purse. It can be a simple goal or a personal affirmation, such as "I create a wonderful life by nurturing my dreams."

It is good to affirm your faith on any day, but it's especially valuable to affirm faith on a day when doubts cloud your mind. Sow in faith and trust that one day you will reap in joy. Wait patiently like a farmer who has sown seeds, letting the natural processes of life bring your garden of faith to perfect fruition in good time.

You can choose an optimistic attitude toward life. Optimism can be cultivated by an act of faith. Faith is a choice, not an argument. Every thought you think colors your experiences, so choose your thoughts carefully. Negative thoughts that hold us back include: I can't, I won't, it's not fair, it won't work, it's too hard, I'm not good enough. Optimistic thoughts help us make positive choices. Choose to replace negative thoughts with positive, empowering thoughts like: I can, it's possible, I'll give it a try, I am able to do this, I can make this work.

Celebrate even a simple baby step of faith, knowing it will lead you to where you need to go. Pray about your plans, hopes, and dreams. Trust that everything can work together to bring you closer to your goal, even when setbacks occur. Whatever the outcome, you'll learn something new and valuable.

Second guessing, trying to control outcomes, or playing it safe can be deadening to the spirit. Take risks and trust. Go ahead and do something you want to do but are afraid to try. Be proactive and leave the final results in God's hands. Overcome your fears by sowing seeds of faith.

Facing Down the Meltdowns

I have experienced my own life crises and survived. When the financial meltdown of 2008 came, I had a meltdown of my own. A combination of health issues, family issues, and the disappearance of work in the publishing industry, freelance writing that had sustained me for almost twenty years, meant that I had trouble paying my bills. Once it had been easy to generate funds through freelance projects, but the publishing industry was in crisis and all work had dried up. It was also nearly impossible to find a day job, even a low-paying one. I faced many challenges during this time.

One of those challenges was keeping my home. When I couldn't pay my mortgage, I applied for a home loan modification. Because I was a freelancer reinventing myself in an industry reinventing itself—and because I couldn't find a day job—I had a lot of explaining to do on my loan application, which was no small task to complete. On January 7, I called my lender to check on the status of my application. The customer service representative said, "Congratulations. You have received the temporary home loan modification and your first payment is due February 1. And your house is in foreclosure and the auction date is February 2."

Trust Life Itself

There are times when even your best efforts fail. Sometimes the most powerful way to deal with a challenge is to stop trying to control events, other people, yourself—and even God. Quit fighting what's happening. Let go of your tight grip and open your hand. Once you admit that you are at the end of your own resources, you make room for life to step in and work a miracle. Unclench your fist and open your hand. Trust life itself to bring what you most need.

I had never been so frightened in my life. I was about to lose my home: I had no money and nowhere to go. However, other forces were at play behind the scenes, and just as buying my home in the first place was a string of miracles, so keeping my home became a string of miracles. A wise friend counseled me to pray and affirm that it was my home and to focus on being in the energy of having it remain my home. This friend had already beaten impossible odds when her husband became ill and they went into financial meltdown. She was able to keep her home in similar circumstances. Friends and family were praying for me. A gift of money from an unexpected source gave me the funds to make the first payment on the modification immediately.

I also received help from a wonderful housing counselor. When I did finally receive my permanent home loan modification, my counselor marveled and told me, "You are a walking miracle. I have never seen anyone in your financial condition get one of these modifications." And so it has gone ever since, as there were more struggles and more miracles manifested in the coming years. I kept my home. My career prospects improved.

Meditate through Your Crisis

I learned some important lessons in facing crises and challenges. The very first was the rock-bottom dependence on God—on a Higher Power. And that is expressed in affirmative prayer when I can think straight. And when I am totally overwhelmed, I meditate. I had been meditating seriously for over a year when this big crisis hit. Though I did rant, rave, and cry when the crisis was upon me, I knew in my bones that anger, fear, and emotional storms would swamp me. I would go into my meditation position and sit until I became clear again. I dropped all judgments of the situation, accepting that it was what it was and that regrets or anticipation were both useless. I moved into the moment and into the deep stillness. Then I took the next step, however small that might have been. I listened for guidance, and guidance came.

Bring into play the almighty power within you, so that on the stage of life you can fulfill your high destined role.
—Paramahansa Yogananda

I practiced staying calm, putting my thoughts in abeyance, focusing only on the moment and on whatever task I had to do. If I woke up in the middle of the night with cold chills of fear in my body and nightmarish scenarios running around in my mind, I released them and meditated myself to sleep again. The only medication I took was meditation and my essential oils to help calm and ground me. My job was to get quiet, listen, do the next step, and trust. No commentary. No excuses. No speculation. No worrying. Just be, set an intention, then do what seemed intuitively appropriate at the moment. Meditate, pray, and serve.

You can also do this in times of crisis. When storms arise, there is a still, small voice that will speak, "Peace, be still." And peace will attend—even in the midst of fear and danger and sorrow. When that peace reigns in your heart, then you can stand, even in the midst of swirling chaos. I have learned that we all have access to that trustworthy inner guidance, but the way we live and the world around us usually drown it out. Train yourself to listen in the quiet times, then you will hear the voice of guidance in the midst of chaos and stress.

If I keep emphasizing the power of affirmative prayer and intention, meditation and staying in the moment, it is because I have experienced it as the center of an authentic power that cannot be moved or shaken. If you can listen and be present and enter that stillness and silence within, then you will find the help you need. You will be transformed within, and if you choose this inner way of life, your outer life will also be transformed. It doesn't have to take a crisis. It will simply be your decision to trust in Something/Someone who is larger than you, and your commitment to hear what whispers in the silence. It is comfort and guidance beyond words, beyond concepts, beyond explanations. If you seek it, you will find it. This sweet, still Presence is always seeking you. I know this with every cell of my being for I have found it to be true in my own life.

Take the Next Step in Faith

An unexpected detour stopped you in your tracks. Losses, lay-offs, deaths, sudden changes—life takes its toll, and you begin to be afraid that the golden highway of life has turned into a dark and dangerous dead end. But a bend in the road is not the end of the road. Sometimes the only thing you can do is take the next step and keep going. Move into a deeper trust and believe that even in this loss you will be shown the way.

Here are some of the affirmations that have helped me in times of crisis:

- There is that within me that knows what to do and how to do it.
- Be still and know that I AM God. Be still and know that I AM.
- Thank You for helping me. Thank You.
- I release. I surrender. No judgment. No attachment.
- I bless this now. This, too, will pass.
- I enter into the Silence. I live in the Presence.
- I am safe. One step at a time. I take no thought. I release.
- God's way is safer than a known way.
- I am enough in this moment. God is my Source.

Remember that you can only control how you respond. You are not responsible for the end result, nor are you responsible for the choices others make. You are only responsible for your thoughts, your attitude, and your actions. Results will vary, as each circumstance is unique; each interrelationship of event, timing, and people involved will create its own solutions.

The solution is inherent in the problem, unfolding moment to moment, choice by choice. How you respond to what is here right now will determine what will be. You are always making choices, and each choice will evolve from the last.

Life is change, growth, loss, and rebirth. So what are you going to do with the one life you have? Focus on the innate wholeness, perfection, and completion of the moment, and on your deepest inner self. Your inner authority not only calms stormy seas, it also sets you free to be spontaneous, flexible, open to new ideas and options. If you can learn to relax your rigid reactions and train yourself to flow with the energy of life, life will unfold with greater ease and grace. You will more easily reflect your essential nature, which knows how to flow with and adapt to the changing seasons of life.

Honor and Bless Memories

There is a sad liberation that comes with loss. It becomes an opportunity to resurrect a new life, a life that may be very different but still can be a good life that blesses others. If you accept the gifts that a new life has to offer, you will honor the old life because you were not afraid to move on in the flow of change.

When inevitable changes come, the old life dies. Summer has its season, autumn has its beauties, and winter will finally come. When the snows of winter bury what's left, we have to accept that life moves on. We can choose to cling to the past, but it does not honor the past. Spring does come. The apple blossoms are eternal. They are always new, yet always the same. Life will not allow us to stand still. Since life itself pushes us forward, let us move forward with grace.

Life is a process of becoming, a combination of states we have to go through. Where people fail is that they wish to elect a state and remain in it.
—Anaïs Nin

As each new season begins, you can choose to honor and bless the memory of what has come before. Your experiences, good and bad, help you learn a deeper appreciation for the changing seasons of life. You can grow and evolve as you, too, make your contribution to the greater good. Choose life knowing that there is a gift of abundance in every moment—if you are willing to look for it. There is new good to create and share. Honor the goodness of the past by choosing to create new possibilities for good now and for the future. If you are still alive, then there is a meaningful contribution you can make to life. Your choices bless and honor the past even as they embrace the possibilities of the future.

Activity: Accept What Is

You can waste a lot of energy fighting the facts. You may be sick or have financial limitations. You might have had a misunderstanding with a friend or loved one. Your job might not be as fulfilling as it once was. Accepting that these conditions exist is not admitting defeat. It is acknowledging what you have to work with. Surrender your disappointment to a Higher Power. Accepting the limitations of human life can be an act of trust, and simply observing what is without judgment can be a powerful inner practice. It is easier to embrace life as it is rather than to continue resisting and rebelling. Your acceptance frees you to trust in the God who can transcend your limitations. Allow room for creative responses to arise instead of holding on tightly to either/or scenarios. Being aware of the realities in a situation helps you cope with difficulties. Like a great ship setting its sails to take advantage of the wind no matter which direction it blows, your life is moved in positive directions by choosing to make the best of whatever comes. When you have faced and accepted what is, you can make wiser choices in every situation.

Three Affirmations

- I get quiet. I trust Life. I take the next step. Grace unfolds.
- God makes a way where there is no way.
- I am guided moment by moment. I am led step by step.

chapter ten

Saying Good-Bye: Loss, Death, and Rebirth

This is what I have learned. Within the sorrow, there is grace. When we come close to those things that break us down, we touch those things that also break us open. And in that breaking open, we uncover our true nature.
—Wayne Muller

Life is filled with paradoxes. Death is a mystery that makes life even more precious. Sorrow can break the heart wide open. As the shell of a seed must be broken open to allow new life to emerge, so we discover that the losses and sorrows we thought would destroy us become the place where new life begins. The round of seasons continually reminds us of death and dormancy, rebirth and resurrection. Autumn's fading glory gives way to the stony gray and sere browns of winter. Then spring emerges in tender green spears and delicate blossoms, merging into the lush growth of the summer's fruitful bounty. The symphony of the seasons is echoed in the seasons of our own lives.

We are all mortal. Nothing lasts forever. When troubles come, we have a choice—let troubles destroy us or transform us. The losses may seem overwhelming, but the love and life at the center of our being are more powerful than any sorrow or darkness.

Bless the pain you feel and the promise of potentialities you cannot see. The human spirit is larger than you yet comprehend, able to transform the unspeakable into a gift to life. Believe that a time of trouble is not an end but a beginning if you are willing to choose life in the midst of your tribulations.

Embrace Life

We can choose to allow life's natural energies to flow in life-giving and supportive ways. When we learn to overcome our fears and access the inner capacity that knows what to do and how to do it, we align ourselves with renewal. Life is change and evolution, and we can choose how we will respond in the midst of life's challenges.

It takes courage to choose life. A small transforming choice multiplied by daily practice and nurtured by continued affirmative thought and prayer can change the trajectory of a life. We often settle for a limited life. Whether it is the well-worn path of family or societal expectations or our own self-doubt and fears that hold us back from more expansive lives, the result is still the same. We end up living lives that may be comfortable and predictable but that never fulfill our potential for greatness. Confronting our mortality and walking through the valley of the shadow of death with a loved one can be a wake-up call, reminding us that as long as we are here living on Earth, we have the power to grow and change.

No matter how much you might like to dig yourself a hole, crawl in, and pull the earth over to cover you like a blanket, you cannot. Life insists on going on. You can choose to numb yourself with addictive behaviors. You can waste a lot of time in denial, pretending that the pain doesn't exist or avoiding the questions you don't want to ask. You can blame others, get angry, and try to deny that there is anything wrong. But a chocolate binge, a drug trip, a tirade against the injustices of life, a hysterical fit, or a plunge into depression eventually leads you back to square one: How do I find meaning in the losses that break my heart? How can I put my life back together again into a healing new pattern?

What makes you feel more alive? What seeds of faith can you sow today that will contribute to life, make things better, express your uniqueness as an individual? Think of what you love. Does the life you live reflect your most authentic priorities? Are you willing to release old limitations and roles to embrace a richer, more deeply satisfying way of being in this world? Instead of allowing grief to overwhelm you, open your arms to life. Have the courage to choose a life you love instead of settling for a pale imitation of the real thing. Be willing to fashion a better world with your mind and hands and heart. Be courageously creative. The courageous choice sets you free. Life is more meaningful and beautiful if you are willing to follow your heart. The life-affirming choice begets life.

Even if you cannot see how conditions can change for the better, trust that your intentional choice begins a chain reaction that will create greater good. Remember that all things are possible, if you dare to believe. Say yes to life right now. Affirm the unseen good that is potentially here. This time of trouble can lead to something meaningful and wonderful if you are willing to look beyond today's shadows and trust that more good awaits. Trust that Infinite Intelligence can make all things work together for the highest good for all if you are willing to do your part. Do you give yourself permission to do what you love? Are you willing to step out in faith and say yes to what you love and yes to life? When you let love lead the way, you allow grace to support you through every season of life.

Sing Your Own Song of Life

Music has always made me feel more alive. It has been at the center of most of the choices I have made that were affirmations of life and expanding possibility. As a little girl, I would dance around the living room to Beethoven's Symphony No. 6, the *Pastoral Symphony*. When I became a teenager, I adored the pop music of the sixties. It was so full of the exuberance and idealism of youth. I enjoyed drama in high school, but when I had to choose between drama and being part of a church choral group, the choral group won. I loved singing in those old Ralph Carmichael, Jimmy Owens, and Kurt Kaiser musicals. I spent another summer in college traveling across the country with the Lutheran Evangelical Movement Gospel Crusaders. I learned to play guitar and sing folk songs. Music grew ever more important in my life over the years. I was a buyer for the music department in a Christian bookstore in the early eighties, which marked a decade that saw the rise of the contemporary Christian music genre. It was a golden era for me as I began cowriting songs and attended the Christian Artists Seminar in Estes Park, Colorado. I found long-term cowriting relationships in Seattle and began a long-distance cowriting relationship with an established Nashville songwriter. I was involved in church and arts organizations and finally chose to move to Nashville in 1993 in pursuit of my musical dreams. Now I have a collection of my own songs, and recording them is part of my dream for future adventures in music.

In fact, it was the music, and my love of music, that moved me into all kinds of wonderful adventures. One reason Nashville has been so transformative for me is that I have found so many kindred spirits who also come alive when they make music. It creates a tight-knit community built around the incomparable "high" of writing songs and performing them for a group of appreciative peers. I have a passion for creating the perfect song, offering a moving performance. I also have a deep appreciation for those who do it well. Nashville is a particularly rich place to hear the best of the best, whether it is at a casual writer's night or a formal performance in a world-class auditorium. Best of all, I am surrounded by people who understand this passion for music, who celebrate excellence, and who feel that life would be dry and dead indeed without making music in one form or another. For me, being involved with music is essential to feeling fully alive. My choice to move to Nashville to follow my musical dreams brought rewards and relationships beyond anything I could have imagined. It also brought its share of heartache and loss. But I still continue to follow that dream by making courageous choices and trusting the inner voice of my heart.

You don't have to be a musician to appreciate the aliveness that music represents. Scientists have confirmed that the nature of the world is musical. The Greeks defined music's most beautiful sounds as arising from certain fixed mathematical relationships—the fingerprints of the gods. Pythagoras, a Greek mathematician, had a school that taught not only the mystery of numbers, but also the use of sound to affect and heal the body, mind, and spirit.

Just as there is a spectrum of light, only part of which we can see, so there is a spectrum of sound. Dolphins can project and receive frequencies more than ten times beyond our limit of hearing. Dogs hear sounds we cannot. In most spiritual traditions, there are many stories of saints, sages, and mystics who sought to cultivate hearing celestial sounds through spiritual practices.

Waves, harmonics, and octaves are some of the ways the electromagnetic spectrum is measured. Johannes Kepler, a seventeenth-century astronomer, believed that each of the planets is alive, inhabited by its own guardian angel, and has its own song. In 1976, two Yale University professors took Kepler's laws and musical notations, fed the information into a computer connected to a synthesizer, and came up with a thirty-minute tape representing one hundred years of planetary motion. The deep structure of music is a reflection of the deep structure of everything else.

If music can bring harmony to the heart and energy to the body, then choose the kind of music that makes you feel most alive. Or choose whatever it is that makes you feel like life is worth living. It could be a career in the arts, running a business, raising a family, working with the land, pursuing a sport, or using your gifts and talents to make the world a better place. Make choices that are deeply resonant with your heart and that lead in the direction of hope. Listen for that which sings within, that which makes you feel more alive. Listen to the music of your heart. Let your choices be in harmony with your highest aspirations. Then, no matter what happens, you will know that you have lived fully and fearlessly.

The Courage to Choose Life

When we struggle through difficult times, we wrestle with questions of "Why me?" and "Why this?" and "Why now?" It takes faith to believe in the outworking of God's intentions for our ultimate good. Doubt and fear can overwhelm us in the face of our own fragility and mortality. It takes great courage to affirm life when loss, sorrow, and death enter our lives. When we choose faith over fear, trusting that God can make a way where there is no way, we can persevere through the changing seasons of life.

If you are in a season of loss, you can still make life-affirming choices. When you are not sure what decision to make, which path to take, or where to invest your life energies, set an intention to live life more fully, no matter what happens. Allow yourself room to grieve your losses, but do not stay locked in your own sorrow. Be positive and proactive. Take care of yourself as you take care of others. Believe the best. Pray and affirm that you are guided and that healing can happen in every circumstance. In tangled situations, trust God to untangle the mess. Be willing to take risks. Dare to embrace life.

Remember that this moment is the point of power. There is nothing you can do about what is past. Your choice here and now is what creates the future. Have the courage to make even one small choice to affirm your faith in life. Even if it seems like your entire world is dying, trust that this winter of the soul will one day become a spring of the spirit. Plant seeds of faith, believing in a resurrection and renewal that is beyond your limited understanding. Surrender to the greater rhythm of life, trusting that your affirmation of life, no matter how weak and trembling it seems in the face of death, does have life-altering power. You may not know when or how renewal will appear. You just have to trust that spring will return in your life.

Concentrate only on what you are able to do today. Let go of trying to control or predict the outcome. Do your best and leave the rest up to God. Trust that a greater process is happening, that all this is working together for your good and your growth. Count difficulties as blessings in disguise, believing that you will one day understand. The courage to keep going may sometimes be the only blessing you can see, but remember that life goes on and reveals its secrets in time. In most of the important things in life, we are dependent on the nature of creation and time, the grace of Divine Love that carries us through the events and processes of living—and dying.

Dying as Sacred Experience

The dying have their own language, a symbolism that often speaks of their life experiences. In their book, *Final Gifts*—a compassionate guide to caring for the gravely ill—hospice nurses Maggie Callanan and Patricia Kelley offer insight into the special awareness that helps the living interpret the communications of the dying. There are parallels between being born and dying, and in hospice the caregivers are in some ways midwives to the process of leaving this world. Just as a midwife helps the mother bring a baby into this world, hospice caregivers help families get through this difficult time of transition. Even in a seemingly dark passage, in this difficult good-bye, there is light, beauty, and blessing to be found.

Dame Cicely Saunders started the modern hospice movement in London in 1967. She said to dying people, "You matter because you are you. You matter until the last moment of your life, and we will do all we can not only to help you die peacefully, but also to live until you die." When it is time to walk with a loved one through the valley of the shadow of death, hospice is there to help the whole family through the process. If you are willing to walk with an open heart into the mystery of death and dying, hospice will teach you how to live.

Every person is unique, and every death has its own story. Though there may not be a clear path through, somehow each step leads to the next, and it is only in looking back that we can see how we were guided so that all things could work together in mysterious ways.

Each one of us is born for a specific reason and purpose, and each one of us will die when he or she has accomplished whatever was to be accomplished. The in-between depends on our own willingness to make the best of every day, of every moment, of every opportunity. The choice is always ours.
—Elisabeth Kübler-Ross

Saying Good-Bye

If you are saying good-bye to a loved one, the sacred dying experience means that it is time to focus on the spiritual even as the loved one's physical body begins to shut down. Loved ones must respect the experience of dying, and while the person who is dying is still alive, we must recognize that it is a process that the living cannot fully understand. Simply acknowledging that death is a spiritual process can be healing for all concerned. It can be a celebration of life as we join hands with the ones we love.

Find Serene Strength Within

You have a secret spring within your heart. It is the hidden gift of inward grace, springing up like an ever-flowing fountain, a deep well that will quench your thirst when life seems like a desert. Moment by moment, this unseen power sustains you through every trouble and trial and through all the changes of a lifetime. Rely on this inner serenity to help you deal with the challenges of life. Grace will appear in your life just when you need it most.

Coping with Physical and Emotional Exhaustion

Dealing with the death of a loved one is hard work, especially for the caregiver. It can leave you emotionally depleted and physically exhausted. If you are a caregiver, allow others to share the burdens and responsibilities and don't feel you have to be responsible for everything. It may be difficult, but try to do your best to replenish yourself by getting plenty of rest and eating well. If possible, do things that relax you and help you stay calm and focused, such as listen to music, meditate, do affirmations, and pray. Make time to be with supportive friends and if that's not enough, consider counseling or a support group

The dying can be teachers to the living. They show us how to make the passage between life and death. And they inspire us to embrace the lives we are given, to live more fully, and to be less afraid. "What, I pray you, is dying?" Saint John Chrysostom asks. "Just what it is to put off a garment. For the body is about the soul as a garment; and after laying this aside for a short time by means of death, we shall resume it again with more splendor."

Celestial Music

Johann Wolfgang von Goethe, the beloved German writer, philosopher, and artist, was born in 1749 and died in 1832. He wrote, "The thought of death leaves me in perfect peace, for I have a firm conviction that our spirit is a being of indestructible nature; it works on from eternity to eternity; it is like the sun, which though it seems to set to our mortal eyes, does not really set, but shines on perpetually." Friends of the dying Goethe heard celestial music in the final hours before his death. Frau von Goethe, the poet's sister-in-law, told a friend: "It's inexplicable! Since dawn yesterday a mysterious music has resounded from time to time, getting into our ears, our bones." Several witnesses compared experiences and confirmed that they, too, were hearing music in different parts of the house. One would hear fragments of a quartet, another a piano, others a choral chant or the sound of an organ or a concertina. It was as if there were heavenly harmonies playing as the poet lay dying. The mysterious music continued until Goethe's last breath.

Celestial music has been heard by others. Saint Thérèse de Lisieux heard celestial music on her deathbed. So did William Blake. John Wesley heard what he thought was the music of angels when he was at the bedside of a dying young woman, and wrote, "I firmly believed that young woman would die in peace; though I did not apprehend it would be so soon. We have had several instances of music heard before or at the death of those that die in the Lord. May we conceive that this is, literally, the music of angels? Can that be heard by ears of flesh and blood?" According to Dr. Joel Funk, a professor of psychology at Plymouth State University in New Hampshire, about 50 percent of those who have had near-death experiences hear music and describe it as a beautiful floating sound.

Hearing music and seeing others who have passed on is common among those who are dying, but only in rare instances do the living share this experience. *Musica universalis*, or music of the spheres, is a medieval philosophical concept that regards the proportions in the movements of the celestial bodies as a form of *musica* (the medieval Latin word for music). The most frequent descriptions of the afterlife portray an unimaginably beautiful land of color, light, and music. A small percentage of those who have survived a near-death experience report visions of inner worlds, paradises, and cities of light with transcendental music. Dante wrote: "The heavens call to you and circle around you, displaying to you their eternal splendors."

Listen to Music

Music can have a profound effect on energy levels and mood. It may even strengthen your immune system. Music can energize with an upbeat rhythm or soothe with mellow sounds. Music expresses the deepest feelings of the human heart. Through the centuries, music has been used to draw people closer to God. Create your own music therapy session by choosing soothing and uplifting music. Let the sound and the spirit of the music heal, comfort, and inspire you.

Musical Therapy

Today, many forms of sound healing are proliferating. Musicians and scientists are exploring the therapeutic value of sound and music. From singing bowls to gongs, chimes, bells, and chanting, ancient traditions are being revived, and new applications for healing with music, vibration, and sound are reemerging as a vehicle for healing, meditation, and self-transformation.

Sound and music can help you process the events of your life, acting as a natural physician in times of stress. Western science has proven what ancient traditions have known for centuries: Sound has the power to heal and to affect the body as well as the mind. Music therapists use music as a healing tool to enhance natural self-healing capacities. Hospitals are using relaxation music to reduce stress and pain in patients. Chanting and singing has been proven to relieve depression. Listening to music uses both the left and right sides of the brain and can influence the frequency of brain waves. Sound is used as an energy medicine by sound healers. Singing bowls and other instruments facilitate meditation and meditative practices. Merely listening to soothing music can help relieve stress and calm your emotions.

Music-thanatology is another one of the ancient wisdoms that has been revived in recent years. The Greeks practiced it; Benedictine monks in the Middle Ages used it. The Music-Thanatology Association International describes it as a musical/clinical modality that unites music and medicine in end-of-life care.

Certified music-thanatologists use harp and voice at the bedside to lovingly serve the dying and their loved ones. This music is not entertainment but therapy that relieves pain, soothes agitation, and helps the patient through the dying process. It is called prescriptive music—live music played in tone and tempo in response to the dying person's needs. The Chalice of Repose Project School of Music-Thanatology in Missoula, Montana, was started by Therese Schroeder-Sheker after she worked in a nursing home and saw the callous treatment of the dying and the dead. A priest suggested she incorporate lines from the sacred scriptures of the world in prayers at patients' bedsides. Music was added, and the concept of music-thanatology and prescriptive music vigils was born.

Music-thanatologists pledge to serve the physical, emotional, and spiritual needs of the dying and acknowledge the inherent worth of each person with unconditional love and attention. They offer an intimate atmosphere of serenity and comfort that can be profoundly healing for the dying, supporting them in their process of releasing earthly life.

Music-thanatology can make a profound difference in the way people experience the end-of-life journey. Encouraging the listener to receive on a deep level, the prescriptive music communicates without words. The harp offers resonant sounds that penetrate the body. The tones of the harp go through the bones. Music-thanatology students learn Gregorian chants and how they affect the body physiologically, as well as prayers and music from many faith traditions. Music creates a sacred space for death to take place or for the family and the patient to process their experience. The sense of hearing is the last to go—even in coma patients. The beauty and harmony of the music reaches past the bodily symptoms and straight to the spirit. The prescriptive live harp music vigils take people beyond the music into a silence that is deeply spiritual and profoundly comforting. No matter what losses you may be grieving, music is a powerful way to connect with the transcendent part of your nature. If the ancients who believed that music and harmony were reflections of the universal order are now being proved correct, you can be assured that music can be a helpful and healing modality for you and for a dying loved one. Sound is vibration, and the right sounds can offer a healing vibration that is felt in the body as well as with the emotions. While walking with a loved one through the valley of the shadow of death or for those mourning after their beloved has passed on, music can provide healing and inspiration.

Music is a reminder that just as there is the tone of a struck note—as well as the unstruck overtones that resonate around that tone—so the events of your life have a struck note, the event of saying good-bye to someone you love deeply. The unstruck notes (the overtones and/or higher harmonics) include grief, loss, and sadness. But there are other harmonics at work that heal and inspire. There is a greater wholeness, a healing energy, and a higher octave of love that is part of the harmonic equation. You may not hear those healing overtones in the first impact of your loss, but they are there, built into the very nature of the universe. You are supported in a sea of sound and vibration. Celestial music has been playing in the background of your life, and going through this passage with a loved one can open your ears to hear the music that has been accompanying you all along.

The Lesson of the Seasons

A tender, fleeting apple blossom is even more beautiful and luminous because it has such a brief appearance. I rejoice in it because it will continue to change and evolve in the life cycle of the apple tree. Winter's bare branches give way to spring's pink and white. Then petals fall like snow and blow away in the wind. Tiny, knobby apple buds appear, and the long, slow days of summer carry the fruit to full perfection. The green leaves of summer turn to russet and brown as the cold weather approaches and the days grow shorter. Autumn brings a red and gold harvest—crisp apples for eating off the tree, apple-sauce, and apple pie for Thanksgiving feasts and golden winter comfort. Looking out the window at the frozen landscape and empty branches covered in snow, I know that those branches will one day be covered in blossom as a new cycle of seasons begins.

Let life be beautiful like summer flowers and death be like autumn leaves.
—Rabindranath Tagore

So it is with the seasons and changes in our lives. You may revel in the innocence of childhood, the joy of schoolchildren discovering childhood classics and favorite games. Though you long to stop the clock and hang onto those moments for just a little longer, you know that loving your child means you must treasure the awkwardness of adolescence, the move to independence, and the assumption of an adult life that may be very different from the fond dreams you had of her future back when she was a baby. A lace wedding dress, a home established farther away than you would like, and, if you are especially blessed, grandbabies: all are part of the growth and evolution of a family. You wouldn't want to keep your child from reaching her full maturity. To control and constrain is to stunt growth.

You can also apply the ideals of parenting to yourself. The ideals may not match the reality you experience, but they can be archetypes of potential that help keep your intention clear in a complicated world. Parent yourself gently in the difficult and challenging times that life brings. One day you will emerge from that season into a happier and more fruitful time. You will understand that the challenges made you strong and drove your roots deeper into the ground of your being.

The hardest winter, the most difficult passage through the valley of the shadow of death, will one day give way to the soft newness of returning spring. Nature teaches the lessons that the heart finds hard to learn. No matter how long the winter, spring always comes with the luminous astonishment of sun and spring flowers. It is not theory or theology that ministers to the broken heart, but presence and power, love and forgiveness, blessing and release.

Give yourself the gift of fully appreciating the seasons of life, moment by moment. And give yourself the gift of allowing yourself and those you love to grow and change and evolve. Trust the wisdom of life to guide you through the changes and losses you encounter, just as you trust that spring will follow winter.

Activity: Invest in a Massage

If you are under stress, especially when caring for others, it's easy to forget to nurture yourself. You cannot serve others well if you are exhausted and overwhelmed. Give yourself permission to get a massage. You deserve it, and you will feel much better afterward. Athletes, dancers, overstressed homemakers, and busy executives have discovered the benefits of therapeutic massage for relieving stress, soothing sore muscles, and enhancing mental and emotional well-being. Invest in your health and you'll reap benefits in mental clarity and emotional calmness. As you invest in your physical well-being, you'll discover more energy for cultivating the spiritual side of life as well. There are many kinds of therapeutic massage available at health spas, clinics, and athletic facilities. You can also do simple self-massage at home. Refresh your feet with peppermint foot lotion, or soothe aching shoulders with a gentle hand massage.

Three Affirmations

- I bless my dearly beloveds and release them with love.
- I listen for celestial music and look for glimpses of heaven on earth.
- God orchestrates my life, and I live in harmony and peace.

chapter eleven

Peace, Be Still: Serene Faith and Grace

It is not in our power to do everything we dream of doing. We must be patient and diligent and hold faithfully before our vision the ideals we serve, no matter how long it may take to accomplish them.
—M. C. Richards

Where do you draw the line between faith and foolishness, confidence and doubt? To admit I struggle with doubts about my own abilities—as well as my ability to create a more abundant life—is not a sign that I am faithless, though it sometimes feels that way. It is a sign that I'm still learning, that I'm even learning to ask better questions that lead me to a larger understanding and a higher consciousness. I may not know all the answers, but I'm becoming wise enough to believe that there is something within me that knows what to do and how to do it. It is wiser than I am. It is not about my control, having all the answers, and being right, but instead about surrender, trust, and copartnering with a greater Presence.

I may not be able to heal myself instantly, lift the weight of current conditions and past poor decisions in one fell swoop, or become everything I wish I could be overnight. But I can become a partner in a greater process, learning to observe what is happening from a higher perspective. As I do that, I open myself to the possibilities of new thoughts, new concepts, and as yet unknown answers that unfold in a timetable that transcends earthly expectations. And because the timetable of my experience unfolds in earth time and space, it comes to me a step at a time—usually baby steps, not giant leaps. However, I cannot assume that the unfolding of a greater reality is limited to my past experience, either. We are talking about transcending expectations as well as meeting or missing them. Faith is practiced in the known—I know this chair will hold me, that the sun comes up every morning, that there is enough air for me to take my next breath—but it is also practiced in the unknown.

The Larger Reality

Wellness comes not by denying the disease but by looking at a larger reality, to an unlimited health and wholeness that lies beyond disease or cure. One can do multiple good things to align with this health and wholeness, such as drink lots of water, rest, eat right, use essential oils, get sun, take medicine, etc. As a yes to the potential for wellness in a body that naturally heals itself, these good choices can be practiced in the expectation (the faith) that they will make a positive difference. Focus on the positive outcome, yet detach from outlining how or when it will unfold. That, too, is an ongoing lesson in an evolving faith. To stay unattached to outcomes and timetables can be challenging, especially when it feels like so much is riding on the results. Have faith in the goodness of God and trust that all things work together for the highest good of all.

Our struggles are sometimes the glory of God working through us in ways we may not understand. When the disciples asked Jesus if the man who was born blind was born that way because his parents sinned or because he sinned, he dismissed the whole question on who was "right" or sinless and who was a sinner and therefore "wrong." He said that the infirmity was to reveal the glory of God. Jesus healed him. And then the blind man saw. (Of course, one also has to remember that the blind man got in hot water with the religious authorities because of this "unorthodox" healing. It didn't fit with their theology and prejudices against Jesus.)

Cultivate Inner Wisdom

The seasons of life offer us insight as we meditate on what we learn and experience. Everything has its time and place. The harvest of youth is achievement; of middle age, perspective; and of old age, wisdom. The psalmist prays, "Teach us to number our days, that we may gain a heart of wisdom." Remember what the heart already knows. Learn from your experiences. Listen for the inner wisdom that is always available to you.

Say Yes to Life

Learn to let your yes be yes, and your no be no. Somewhere along the continuum between wholeness and brokenness, health and illness, prosperity and poverty, abundance and lack, we progress in conscious understanding through choice (of both faith and practice). As we grow in awareness, the very thing we struggle with has the potential to be the gateway to the freedom we desire. Sometimes we have to know what we don't want before we can understand what we truly want, what we are not before we can become more fully our true selves. Say yes to life. Listen for life's answering yes.

Learn a Lesson from Dogs

You're strolling in the park. And here comes Fido, straining at the leash, sniffing and snuffling and oh so happy to be out in the fresh air. Canine enthusiasm is unlimited. Dogs love life wholeheartedly, adoringly, without reservation or judgment, greeting each new scent or sight with boundless joy and radiant, unself-conscious glee. Take note of this exuberant enthusiasm and apply it to your own attitude in life. Appreciate and receive whatever the moment offers.

When you fail to live up to your ideals, remember that every stage of growth can be lived in integrity and have its unique challenges met. Just because a sixth-grader has only sixth-grade math skills doesn't mean that he won't study calculus when he is a senior in high school. A toddler repeatedly falls on the living room floor and gets up again and again. One day that toddler will be an adult, capable of climbing a mountain, running in a marathon, or just walking across the living room without falling down. The toddler is whole, perfect, and complete in the toddler stage. The sixth-grader is whole, perfect, and complete in his understanding of age-appropriate math. You are continually growing and evolving into higher stages of competency and understanding. And that includes a greater understanding of faith and integrity. It expands as you grow, taking one more step of faith in this moment, without attaching it to results. You take the next step, and it doesn't matter whether you do it perfectly or not. What matters is that you make yourself available to the process of growth.

There is nothing that persuades us or pushes us or forces us to create faith. Faith means tranquility, and complete tranquility is the source of our nature and existence.
—Dainin Katagiri

Recognize your union with God. God is good, and that good expresses in, through, and for you to produce life, health, understanding, growth, and wholeness. As consciousness expands, you will more fully express the Divine in your thoughts, actions, and experiences. You can live in a higher harmonic of serenity, abundance, and joy. Walk in faith. Affirm the good in life, and take the next step in faith. Release attachment to results, and trust that the Presence of God is with you, within you, behind and before you.

Recognize Your Spiritual Magnificence

Most of us do not recognize our own greatness and potential. We are filled with love, but most of us do not know it. Like a natural spring that has been overloaded with garbage that stops the water from flowing, so our lives become cluttered and blocked by the refuse of our own poor choices, as well as our poor responses to the choices of others, which have added to our burden of guilt and despair. But there is that within us that knows what to do, is greater than all our mistakes, is able to move us beyond the frustrating circumstances that seem to rule our lives.

We can set that inner power in motion by thinking different thoughts and making new choices. It is the new choices made consciously that help us clear the clutter, remove the refuse, and open the way for the fountain of life-giving water to flow again. The water has always been available. We are the ones who closed it off with our unconscious and poor choices, and only we can open that inner spring again with better choices.

Set your intentions for the good, aim toward wholeness and health, and you will be aligning yourself with the natural forces of the universe. This is the true meaning of being in the will of

God. It is not a forced decision against our own natures, but a recognition that the harmony and order of all of creation is in tune with the love of God, and we are meant to be a part of that beautiful music. God is love, and so are you. Choose to live in that love and allow the loving nature of God to express itself in all facets of your life.

You will discover that when you cease resisting the good and allow it to flow in your life, the very goodness and greatness of the nature of creation will respond, leading you and even carrying you in unexpected ways to ever greater good. Synchronicity, or Divine timing, will appear more frequently in your life, bringing resources, people, events, and opportunities together in ways that may sometimes feel miraculous.

Whatever your spiritual beliefs or theological background, it is enough for now that you begin to understand that you are not alone in a cold and meaningless universe, but that you are part of a very personal yet impartial spiritual whole that includes all that is created—and all that is uncreated. You are a portal where the infinite potential of God becomes the finite reality of human experience. And as you learn to trust that Higher Power, that something greater within, you will tap into the energies of love and the pulsating harmony of the life force within.

When you focus on and lean into that Presence of God within, you move beyond the confines of your current situation. Instead of limitation, doubt, fear, anger, and frustration, you tap into a sense of freedom and possibility. Even a feeling or an image of the vastness of eternity can help you move beyond your fears into an experience of faith and hope. Imagine a panoramic view of mountain, ocean, prairie, or any awe-inspiring landscape, then imagine that the quality of your very being is made more expansive simply by contemplating such beauty. Go out on a clear night and gaze up at the stars. Remember that you are a part of this infinite beauty and that it reflects your own nature back to you. Moving to a higher level of understanding and consciousness, you begin to move beyond the small self of fear, limitation, addiction, and old ways of thinking into a more open and receptive place.

Using the Power within to Cultivate Peace

There is that within us that knows what to do and how to do it. The part of us that knows is a part of the Greater Consciousness. Reaching out beyond the boundaries of time and space, we open our hearts and minds to the infinite possibilities that exist in the Mind of God. Through imagination, visualization, and choosing new thoughts and actions, we can create a new reality in our lives. There is a higher self that believes and knows more than our limited consciousness can encompass.

You don't have to *get* the power; you *are* the power, deeply connected to the Divine, with the essence of the Divine within. When you set an intention, you are choosing the direction you want your life to unfold, and the energies of God will flow through you in that direction. Your consciousness creates and coordinates with the infinite field of possibilities.

When you have done what you know to do, it's time to let a Higher Power do the rest. Let go of your agendas and stop trying to second-guess how things will come together. On this spiritual path, you are not depending on your own resources or limited understanding. You have chosen to believe that God is your Source. While you must do your best with what you know to do, it is up to God, to make it happen. Your conscious choice sets things in motion, but it is the unseen that works to pull it all together. Trust the process, knowing that all things work together for the highest good. Recognize that the unlimited Mind of God knows far more than your limited human mind.

You'll discover that the Divine orchestrates the answers to your prayers and affirmations in ways you cannot imagine or predict.

Make a conscious choice to cultivate peace and happiness in your heart. Resolve to find reasons to rejoice rather than reasons to complain. Make gratitude a way of life. Pay attention to the simple, small, wonderful gifts the universe brings into your life every day, like hot showers, a car that runs, a job to do, friends and colleagues to see, and good food to eat. See each person as a Divine appointment to be greeted with kindness and love. Every circumstance has its mercies and small blessings. When you praise the goodness of life, you inspire faith in your heart and teach your soul to trust. Develop a habit of being thankful in the good times, so those habits of gratitude and faith will be well established when the difficult times arise.

Each Day Is a Gift

Accept each day—even the gloomy difficult ones—as a gift. Focus on reasons to be grateful. Your gratitude will color your attitude and help you stay focused on the infinite possibilities of grace unfolding in your life. Release your expectations, do your best, be grateful, and watch what unfolds. When you apply simple spiritual principles to the choices you make and the thoughts you think, you can create a meaningful and fulfilling life.

Follow your heart, and it will lead you to where you need to go. The heart is wiser than the head. Though you need to pay attention to the logic of the mind, when it comes to the most important choices in life, the heart's wisdom will guide you most surely. Value the wisdom of your body. Honor the people in your life. Be generous with your heart and offer others compassion instead of judgment, kindness instead of indifference, and encouragement instead of criticism. Love is not a commodity to be hoarded but a blessing to be shared. When you are rooted deeply in Divine Love, you have access to a boundless supply of energy, joy, hope, and peace. The more love you give away, the more returns to you and the more there is to go around.

Prayer is a natural part of connecting to the help and wisdom that is available from a greater Source. Speaking to God naturally and trustingly, like a child confiding to a parent, is one form of prayer. Affirmative prayer takes this one step further, helping you become a cocreator with a Higher Power and take a more active role as partner in bringing forth the potential of a more expansive life. Here are three simple steps for affirmative prayer:

1. State that God is the Source of all that is and that God is your Source.
2. Describe what you desire as if it is already so, using the present tense. Use affirmations and statements of faith that describe what you want to create or experience.
3. Be grateful right now and trust that the Divine is working all things together for the highest good.

Using affirmations in the first person, present tense, speaks to the part of our mind, the subconscious, that lives beyond time and space in the eternal here, the forever now. That part of us which is beyond time and space responds, creating a new reality in mysterious and wonderful ways that can sometimes feel like miracles. How this happens cannot be predicted, because it is the job of the eternal spiritual part of you, connected to God, to put that together. Say to yourself, "I know what. God knows how."

Align with Spiritual Realities

Be fully present in the miracle of this day. Being fully present in the here and now has great liberating potential, helping you discern the real and lasting in the midst of the distracting and temporary. Thoreau wrote, "In eternity there is indeed something true and sublime. But all these times and places and occasions are now and here. God himself culminates in the present moment, and will never be more divine in the lapse of all the ages." I believe you don't have to travel to a mystic mountaintop or sail across the seven seas to find this treasure. I believe it is already within you and accessible in the life you already lead.

To offer no resistance to life is to be in a state of grace, ease, and lightness. This state is then no longer dependent upon things being in a certain way, good or bad.
—Eckhart Tolle

Ask yourself what you can do to stay connected to a greater awareness and to bring a sense of presence and attention to the life you lead today. What does it mean to live in such a way that you experience yourself and others as expressions of the Divine? If the ancient saying "As above, so below" is true, how can you bring heaven to earth—and is it possible to find the eternal in the temporal, heaven on earth as well as above? How do you discover and nurture serenity in your daily life?

Cultivate alignment with a greater spiritual reality, the hidden rhythm of universal love expressing itself through creation and in human hearts. If you are willing to live with the questions, enter the silence, listen with all your senses, and surrender to love, you will discover that there are no ordinary people, no ordinary places, and grace is at the center, a hidden presence that is available to all. Drawing on the deep wisdom of the timeless and eternal, you will discover that your daily round of errands, laundry, meetings, work, relationships, and social obligations begin to partake of the attributes of timelessness, peace, and even eternal bliss. A serene and fulfilling life can emerge as the fruit of your thoughts, choices, beliefs, and attitude.

Activity: Focus on the Good

What you think about colors your experience of life. Your ability to focus your awareness is a wonderful tool for creating positive change in your perceptions. You can choose to create a better life on a thought-by-thought basis. If you focus on what you dislike, what makes you angry, and whom you disagree with, you'll find that your mind will dwell on those negative thoughts. You can change your focus and choose to think about what is good and true and beautiful. Focus your thoughts on the good in a situation or a person and your mind naturally looks for more good. Consciously choose to look at everything, even difficult people or unpleasant situations, as if there is a hidden blessing to be found. Affirm that even the most stressful situation offers a hidden blessing and that a deeper truth lies behind the changing circumstances you find yourself experiencing. Be grateful for the good that is in your life. Accept each day as a gift. Cultivate a thankful heart. You find what you look for, so focus on reasons to be grateful. Your gratitude will help you develop a more positive and life-affirming attitude.

Three Affirmations

- Every right desire of my heart is filled with ease and grace.
- My heart is at peace, my mind is at rest.
- It is all God and it is all good; all things work together for the highest good.

Part Four

Serenity through the Seasons of Life

If the day and night are such that you greet them with joy, and life emits a fragrance like flowers and sweet-scented herbs, is more elastic, more starry, more immortal—that is your success.
—Henry David Thoreau

chapter twelve

Celebrating Serenity All Year Round: A Collection of Practical Tips

To be interested in the changing seasons is a happier state of mind than to be hopelessly in love with spring.
—George Santayana

Throughout the year, you want to enjoy as many simple seasonal celebrations as possible to make your life more serene: gather fall leaves, build a snowman, pick a spring bouquet, light sparklers, have a summer picnic, visit a farmers market. Celebrate the seasons of life by bringing people together. For instance, celebrate the first day of spring with a tea party or host a fall harvest potluck on the night of the big football game. Decorate your home with fall pumpkins, winter evergreens, or spring flowers. You don't have to limit yourself to birthdays and holidays when you want to celebrate with a friend. Create your own special occasions and celebrate life together. These may be spur-of-the moment meetings or planned festivities, but with good friends, even just being together can be a special occasion. Celebrate a raise, a promotion, or the accomplishment of some cherished goal. Celebrate the first rose in bloom, the first day of summer vacation, the first tomato from your garden, the last rose of summer, the last day before school begins, the last day of the year. Gather your earthier friends to have a drumming circle beneath a full moon. Enjoy an Oscar night dessert party. Choose an unconventional holiday like Groundhog Day as an excuse to invite others over to share a special meal and watch the movie *Groundhog Day*. Enjoy the round of the seasons by sharing the high points with friends and family.

Whatever your preference or mood, use the following suggestions as inspiration to also create your own private celebrations to savor the gifts that every season brings.

Spring

Spring has returned. The earth is like a child that knows poems.
—Rainer Maria Rilke

1. Plant a Tree
Planting a tree is an act of faith that expresses a deep hope for the future. It can be a gift to your children and your children's children. Johnny Appleseed planted apple trees across the frontier, knowing that future generations would enjoy them. Timber companies plant trees, knowing that they will be harvested thirty, forty, or a hundred years from now. Plant a tree—or a seed, if you don't have space for a tree. Make it a tangible symbol of a seed of faith you're planting in your heart.

2. Speak Encouraging Words
Words are important. The things you say can inspire, encourage, and uplift. They can be agents for harm or agents for healing.

Speaking encouraging words doesn't take much effort, but it does take a conscious decision. Your choice to speak kind words will cause positive seeds of hope to be sown in the lives of others. Gentle words can soothe a troubled spirit and smooth out tangled relationships. Just as small seeds can grow into tall trees, those few kind words can grow into a lasting legacy of love.

3.   Be a Child for a Day

The wise person understands that childhood goes to the roots of your soul. Children have wisdom that adults have forgotten. Reclaim your childlike wisdom and pretend to be a child for a day. If you don't remember how to be a child, invite a youngster to spend the day with you. Indulge in favorite childhood activities. Go to the zoo, roll in the grass, or play with other children. Have a day of pure fun. Think about ways you can cultivate a childlike spirit, imagination, and openness.

4.   Put Your House in Order

View spring cleaning as a healing ritual. Cleaning house is like cleansing and ordering your life. You can ignore clutter, but it is still a distraction, like a squeaky wheel or dripping faucet. Create an oasis of restful cleanliness and order in your home. Use your housecleaning time to put your thoughts in order, too. There is something about repetitive work that allows the mind to think more clearly, and cleaning house can be symbolic of other cleansing and ordering in your life.

5.   Stop and Smell the Roses

Do you take the time to enjoy life's bountiful gifts? A dewy rose smiles at you from a neighbor's garden. Daisies dance by the roadside as you drive to work. A planter full of impatiens colors the entrance to the bank. An unfolding bud or a colorful flower is a sign of grace in the midst of a busy day. Bury your nose in a fragrant blossom and let the day's stresses melt away. Buy a single rose and place it in a vase on your desk at work. Let it remind you to savor the beauty of life.

Summer

Summer is the time when one sheds one's tensions with one's clothes, and the right kind of day is jeweled balm for the battered spirit. A few of those days and you can become drunk with the belief that all's right with the world.
—Ada Louise Huxtable

1.   Enjoy Summer Abundance
Summer ripe tomatoes can never be duplicated by card-board-flavored winter supermarket tomatoes. When fruits and vegetables are in season, they deliver fabulous flavor at the low-est prices. And so it is with life as well. Savor the long days and summer heat. Listen to cicadas sing. Watch your garden flourish and follow the path of the sun as it arcs through the sky every day. Enjoy fruit when it's at its peak and be thankful in whatever weather a day offers. Go on a summer picnic. Light sparklers on the Fourth of July. Go diving in the local swimming hole. Pick wildflowers. Take a nap on a lazy afternoon.

2.   Take a Soul Vacation
There are vacations—and then there are soul vacations. A soul vacation can happen in a few minutes, a few hours, or a few days. Instead of packing your bags and heading for distant desti-nations, you can indulge your imagination, spend some time in contemplation, and satisfy your soul with the honey sweetness of the present moment. A soul vacation makes much of small things. Enjoy a good book that takes you on inner adventures.

Watch a bee browse in the heart of a flower, or stroke a cat's soft fur. Take a walk in the woods. Sit and think about life.

3. Breathe Deeply

Babies breathe naturally and easily, filling their lungs with air and releasing the breath fully. As adults, we often lose that sense of ease and openness, breathing more shallowly, restricting the inflow and outflow of breath. Do you take quick, shallow breaths? This kind of breathing creates tension. Take a gentle deep breath, feeling it reach down toward your belly. Exhale with an audible sigh. Did you feel your body relax as you exhaled? Spend ten minutes breathing gently and deeply, allowing the breath to relax and refresh you.

4. Be a Tourist in Your Hometown

Do you appreciate the place where you live? Do you know its history? Where would you go if you wanted to show an out-of-town friend the local sights? If you travel hundreds of miles to see the sights of some other part of the country but neglect the treasures waiting for you in your own backyard, you are missing out on wonderful adventures. Visit the tourist attractions in your own city and explore the sights. Visit a local museum, a favorite restaurant, a park, or a historical sight. You may be surprised by what you'll find!

5. Go Barefoot in the Grass

When Moses encountered the burning bush, the Lord told him to take off his shoes for he was standing on holy ground. You may not be confronted by a burning bush or hear a Voice from heaven, but you can choose to see common earth as holy ground. Children find wonder in simple things, like soft green grass and squishy mud. Get in touch with your inner child. Take your shoes off and go barefoot in the grass. Or paddle your feet in a mud puddle. Or feel the sand between your toes. Revel in the tactile sensation of the good earth beneath your feet.

Fall

Autumn is the eternal corrective. It is ripeness and color and a time of completion; but it is also breadth, and depth, and distance. What man can stand with Autumn on a hilltop and fail to see the span of his world and the substance of the rolling hills that reach to the far horizon?
—Hal Borland

1.   Sing in the Rain

The day may be gloomy with dark clouds and showers. Your mood might match the day. Light the fires of your heart with a chant of praise, a hymn of wonder, or even a funny doo-wop song that makes you laugh. You don't have to be a great singer to enjoy the benefits of making music. When you sing, your whole body resonates with the sound. You take deeper breaths and get more oxygen into your system. Singing can give your spirit a lift. The music will bring sunshine into your soul.

2.   Have a Good Cry

A stiff upper lip and holding your emotions in are highly over-rated. Nature has a built-in tension reliever for both men and women, and it starts with a willingness to cry and to allow those deeply felt emotions to surface. Tears can be healing. When life is stressful, or pain and sorrow seem overwhelming, the best prescription might be a good cry. If a moody rain is falling, let your tears overflow like the healing water dropping from heavy clouds. When the storm has passed, you may even see a rainbow shining through those tears.

3. Get Out in the Fresh Air

If you've been closeted indoors too long, your thoughts get as stuffy as the closed rooms you've been living in. It's time to get out and let the wind blow through your hair, the sun shine on your face, and the fresh air invigorate your attitude. Let the glorious colors of autumn remind you that life is larger and airier and freer than the enclosed world you've been immured in. Watch a squirrel scrambling through leaves, intent on her business. Gather colorful leaves to take home. Nature shares secrets of renewal with those who will take time to listen to her.

4. Appreciate Art

The soul longs for beauty and to express itself through beauty. Art, architecture, music, and human creativity express the soul of the artist. Artists teach us to really see life, capturing the moment so we can meditate on it again and again. Cultivate an appreciation of art. It will enrich your life, expand your understanding, and feed your soul. Enjoy a trip to an art museum, hang meaningful pictures on your walls, take a class in art appreciation. Make art an essential part of your life. It will nurture your soul. Practice art as meditation: Make a collage, paint or draw, and express yourself through creativity.

5. Seek Serendipity

Serendipity is the ability to find valuable or agreeable things not sought after. Cultivate an attitude of faith and optimism. Be flexible and spontaneous. Explore a specialty shop that intrigues you, such as a fabric store, hardware store, spa or salon, travel store, candle shop, or import store. If something intrigues you or draws your attention, explore that interest. It may lead you to a whole new adventure. Appreciate delightful surprises that remind you the world is large and you never know what a day will bring forth.

Winter

Sometimes our fate resembles a fruit tree in winter. Who would think that those branches would turn green again and blossom? But we hope it, we know it.
—Johann Wolfgang von Goethe

1. Dream by the Fire
Dusk is settling in, and the evening lights are coming on. The hearth glows with the warmth of the fire, and you are comfortably ensconced in an armchair or cushioned by soft pillows. It is a time for dreaming and allowing the cares of the day to fall away. Let yourself dream by the fire. Build a warm fire on a winter evening. If you don't have a fireplace, create a cozy atmosphere with low lamplight, candles, and comfortable cushions. Let body and soul take time out for contemplative rest and renewal.

2. Choose Uplifting Entertainment
Make better entertainment choices, especially in winter when there are not as many outdoor activities available. Choosing entertainment alternatives that lift your spirits and encourage you to be a better person will give you extra energy and enhance your spiritual life. Your entertainment choices color your mood and affect your attitude. Inspiring entertainment makes you feel better about life. When you want to watch something on TV, look for programs that inform as well as entertain. Better yet, get away from passive entertainment altogether and create your own fun with friends and family.

3. Make a Pot of Soup
Making soup is a very comforting thing to do. There's something soothing about chopping vegetables, simmering broth,

adding herbs, and tasting the alchemical transformation of common ingredients simmered together. When you make soup, you are transforming simple veggies and broth into an ambrosial and sustaining meal that feeds the body and nourishes the soul. Buy the best of autumn bounty from the vegetable stand. Enjoy the simple delights of homemade soup.

4.   Take a Winter Walk

Bundle up for whatever weather is going on outside and take yourself out for a winter walk. Even if the weather outside is frightful, a winter walk can be delightful. Getting outside is good for body and soul. Stretch your legs and enjoy the outline of bare branches against a winter sky. Take delight in the crunch of snow under your feet and catch snowflakes on your tongue during snowstorms. Before you leave, prepare hot chocolate or hot spiced cider to welcome you home and warm you after your winter expedition.

5.   Repair or Restore Something

Take advantage of all that indoor time to do a little mending and restoring. Pick one simple project to restore, repair, or renew. Enjoy the process of creating something useful or beautiful out of broken things. You can reupholster an old chair, refinish a table, repair a favorite piece of clothing, or restore some discarded treasure to its rightful place of honor and use. Ply your needle, sand the surface of the wood, or paint a bright new color on a dingy, faded wall with mindful attention and gratitude.

Christmas and the Holiday Season

Winter is the time for comfort, for good food and warmth, for the touch of a friendly hand, and for a talk beside the fire: it is the time for home.
—Dame Edith Sitwell

1.   Simplify Your Celebration

Informal get-togethers and spur-of-the-moment celebrations encourage lightness of spirit and spontaneity. Invite a friend over for a cup of coffee and some cookies or host a potluck dessert evening. Instead of feeling overwhelmed by elaborate preparations, you can enjoy spending time with loved ones and nibbling festive goodies made by other hands. If you want to invest more time in enjoying friends than in elaborate preparations, create a more casual celebration.

2.   Beat the Holiday Blues

Though the Christmas season is filled with joyous celebration, the holiday blues can make life miserable for some people. The expectation of a happy, perfect holiday may not be the reality you experience. The painful contrast of losses and sorrows, and even life's little disappointments, can bring on the dark fog of depression in the midst of a sparkling celebration. If you want to beat the holiday blues, make plans to head them off before they begin. Take care of yourself. Get plenty of sleep. Take a brisk walk outdoors. Don't forget that daily exercise energizes you and raises your spirits. Eat well instead of grabbing fast food. When you're feeling overextended, cut back on activities and take time to nurture yourself. Let the simple pleasures of the Christmas season remind you of how much good there is in life.

3.   Choose the Comfort of the Familiar

Take pleasure in familiar rituals at Christmas. Find joy in old family customs, and let soothing reminders of Christmases past comfort your heart today. Though new experiences are wonderful, there's something deeply nurturing about the old, familiar ways. Go out to see the colorful holiday lights and decorations. Share a cup of hot cocoa with a friend. Wrap presents and put them under the tree, even if it's a tiny tabletop tree. Call family if you can't visit. Bake the family Christmas cookie recipe. You don't have to re-create the old holiday extravaganzas, but do one small thing to remind you of past seasonal joys.

4. Leave Room in Your Schedule

When you're tempted to pack your days with too many activities and too many people, deliberately mark out some empty space in your calendar. If you have a tight schedule one day, balance it the next day with a more flexible and open schedule. Take life as it comes and you'll weather its tempests more easily. Colds and flu may force you to take a needed time of rest. Sometimes cuddling up with a comforter and taking a nap is more important than trying to squeeze another event into your life.

5. Decorate Naturally

Forgo the tacky plastic ornaments and bizarrely blinking aluminum trees. Instead, rediscover the gentle magic of natural-looking arrangements made from greens and flowers. Choose a tree for its personality instead of its perfection. Exchange the usual sheared tree for a live tree that can be planted after Christmas. Intersperse evergreen arrangements with ornaments and candles. Use them in floral arrangements. Put twinkling lights on the Christmas tree, light tapers that will shine like living stars in the house, and let dark windows reflect the warm glow of firelight in a cozy living room.

Conclusion

Serene Presence

God, give us grace to accept with serenity the things that cannot be changed, courage to change the things which should be changed, and the wisdom to distinguish the one from the other.
—Reinhold Niebuhr

Finding Serenity in Seasons of Stress is a journey, not a destination. Consider this book a map of the territory, not the territory itself. Stress is unavoidable in modern life. Serenity is like an oasis in the midst of changes and challenges, offering a way to become more conscious in your choices and attitudes. Each person's journey is unique, so what may work for one person may be inappropriate advice for another. Trust your own instincts, for that inner voice will guide you in wonderful and often unexpected ways.

Remember that meditation is an essential tool that can bring calm and focus to your life. It is one of the core skills for creating a more serene life. Experiment with different forms of meditation to see what feels right and works for you. I have listed some of my favorite books on meditation from many faith traditions in the bibliography as a starting point.

Set an intention to cultivate more serenity in your heart, and you will be surprised by the ways serenity makes its way into your daily life. You will also be challenged to make changes that may be far beyond the scope of merely reducing stress in your life. Creating a calming home atmosphere, getting grounded and centered in your body, and being proactive about making positive incremental changes will help you create a more tranquil and meaningful existence.

Serenity is not the absence of stress but an openness to experiencing a greater sense of the Divine Presence in your life. You will be guided as you discover ways to blend spirituality and practicality to uncover the hidden wholeness that is already within. *Finding Serenity in Seasons of Stress* offers encouragement and simple ideas to create a happier and more blessed life. May it be a reminder of the stillness and aliveness that are at the center of your being.

If this book has helped you connect to God as your Source of peace, love, and abundance, then it has done what I intended it to do. As you discover your own spiritual magnificence, you will live more and more from an inner serenity that can heal the world. The serene spirit is more able to give love, and love, in the end, is the point of life. May you be blessed on your journey. May love, joy, and peace be evermore fully expressed in each moment.

That exquisite poise of character which we call serenity is the last lesson of culture; it is the flowering of life, the fruitage of the soul. It is precious as wisdom, more to be desired than gold—yea, than even fine gold. How insignificant mere money seeking looks in comparison with a serene life—a life that dwells in the ocean of Truth, beneath the waves, beyond the reach of tempests, in the Eternal Calm!

—James Allen

Bibliography and Resources

These are just a few of the inspirations I have drawn from. I hope this list will introduce you to wonderful writers to inspire you on your journey. Books and resources are listed by chapter topic.

Part One: The Heart of Serenity

Strong, Mary. *Letters of the Scattered Brotherhood: A Twentieth-Century Classic for Those Seeking Serenity and Strength*. San Francisco: HarperSanFrancisco, (1948) 1991.

Chapter One: Serenity Is a Choice

Benson, Bob Sr. and Michael W. Benson. *Disciplines for the Inner Life*. Nashville: Thomas Nelson, 1989.

Briggs, John and F. David Peat. *Seven Life Lessons of Chaos: Spiritual Wisdom from the Science of Change*. New York: HarperCollins, 1999.

Jones, Dennis Merritt. *The Art of Being: 101 Ways to Practice Purpose in Your Life*. New York: Tarcher/Penguin, 2008.

Chapter Two: Coming Home to Serenity

Alexander, Christopher. *The Nature of Order: An Essay on the Art of Building and the Nature of the Universe, Book 4 – The Luminous Ground*. New York: Routledge, 2004.
(website: www.natureoforder.com)
————. *The Timeless Way of Building*. New York: Oxford University Press, 1979.
(website: www.livingneighborhoods.org/ht-0/bln-exp.htm)
Alexander, Christopher, Sara Ishikawa, Murray Silverstein. *A Pattern Language: Towns, Buildings, Construction*. New York: Oxford University Press, 1977.
(website: www.patternlanguage.com)
Messervy, Julie Moir. *The Inward Garden: Creating a Place of Beauty and Meaning*. Boston: Little, Brown & Company, 1995.
(website: www.jmmds.com)
Moran, Victoria. *Shelter for the Spirit: How to Make Your Home a Haven in a Hectic World*. New York: HarperCollins, 1998.
Stoddard, Alexandra. *Gracious Living in a New World: Finding Joy in Changing Times*. New York: HarperCollins, 1997.
Susanka, Sarah. *The Not So Big House: A Blueprint for the Way We Really Live*. Newtown, CT: Taunton Press, 2009.
(websites: www.susanka.com and www.notsobighouse.com)
Susanka, Sarah. *The Not So Big Life: Making Room for What Really Matters*. New York: Random House, 2007.
(website: www.notsobiglife.com)

Chapter Three: Serene Healing: The Wisdom of the Body

Andrews, Barry M. (ed.). *A Dream Too Wild: Emerson Meditations Every Day of the Year*. Boston: Skinner House Books, 2004.

Emerson, Ralph Waldo. *The Spiritual Emerson: Essential Works by Ralph Waldo Emerson.* New York: Tarcher/Penguin, 2008. (website of complete works of Emerson: www.rwe.org)

Faulds, Richard. *Kripalu Yoga: A Guide to Practice On and Off the Mat.* New York: Bantam Books, 2006.

Jahnke, Roger. *The Healer Within: Using Traditional Chinese Techniques to Release Your Body's Own Medicine.* New York: HarperCollins, 1997.

Maurine, Camille and Lorin Roche. *Meditation Secrets for Women: Discovering Your Passion, Pleasure, and Inner Peace.* New York: HarperCollins, 2001.

Phillips, Jan. *Divining the Body: Reclaim the Holiness of Your Physical Self.* Woodstock, VT: Skylight Paths, 2005.

Schiffmann, Erich. *Yoga: The Spirit and Practice of Moving into Stillness.* New York: Pocket Books, 1996.

Stapleton, Don. *Self-Awakening Yoga: The Expansion of Consciousness through the Body's Own Wisdom.* Rochester, VT: Healing Arts Press, 2004.

Whicher, Stephen E. (ed.). *Selections from Ralph Waldo Emerson.* Rolling Meadows, IL: Riverside/Houghton Mifflin, 1960.

Chapter Four: Serene Spirit: Meditation and Mindfulness

Hanh, Thich Nhat. *The Miracle of Mindfulness: A Manual on Meditation.* Boston: Beacon Press, 1996. (website: www.plumvillage.org)

Kabat-Zinn, Jon. *Wherever You Go, There You Are: Mindfulness Meditation in Everyday Life.* New York: Hyperion, 2005.

Jon Kabat-Zinn at the Center for Mindfulness Mindfulness-Based Stress Reduction Program, University of Massachusetts Medical School (website: www.umassmed.edu/cfm/stress/index.aspx)

Khan, Pir Vilayat Inayat. *Awakening: A Sufi Experience*. New York: Tarcher/Putnam, 1999.

Martin, Philip. *The Zen Path through Depression*. San Francisco: HarperSanFrancisco, 1999.

Merton, Thomas. *New Seeds of Contemplation*. New York: New Directions, 2007.

Merton, Thomas. *The Springs of Contemplation: A Retreat at the Abbey of Gethsemani*. Notre Dame, IN: Ave Maria Press, 1997.

Pennington, M. Basil. *Centering Prayer: Renewing an Ancient Christian Prayer Form*. New York: Image Books, 2001.

Part Two: Serene Relationships

Zander, Rosamund Stone and Benjamin Zander. *The Art of Possibility: Transforming Professional and Personal Life*. New York: Penguin Books, 2002.

Chapter Five: Love, Honor, and Cherish: Serenity Begins with You

Cameron, Julia. *The Vein of Gold: A Journey to Your Creative Heart*. New York: Tarcher/Putnam, 1 997.

Muller, Wayne. *Sabbath: Restoring the Sacred Rhythm of Rest*. New York: Bantam, 1999.

Orloff, Judith. *Positive Energy: 10 Extraordinary Prescriptions for Transforming Fatigue, Stress, and Fear into Vibrance, Strength, and Love*. New York: Three Rivers Press, 2004.

Stoddard, Alexandra. *Tea Celebrations: The Way to Serenity*. New York: William Morrow, 1994.

Chapter Six: Playful Serenity: Enjoying Life Together

Kabat-Zinn, Myla and Jon Kabat-Zinn. *Everyday Blessings: The Inner Work of Mindful Parenting*. New York: Hyperion, 1997.

Levine, Stephen and Ondrea Levine. *Embracing the Beloved: Relationship as a Path of Awakening*. New York: Anchor Books, 1996.

Orloff Judith. *Emotional Freedom: Liberate Yourself from Negative Emotions and Transform Your Life*. New York: Harmony Books, 2009.

Chapter Seven: Joyful Service: The Beloved Community

Horwitz, Claudia. *The Spiritual Activist: Practices to Transform Your Life, Your Work, a nd Your World*. New York: Penguin, 2002.

Martin Luther King Jr. Center for Nonviolent Social Change (website: www.thekingcenter.org/king-philosophy)

Winton-Henry, Cynthia with Phil Porter. *What the Body Wants: From the Creators of Interplay*. Winfield, BC: Northstone, 2004.

Chapter Eight: Bringing Your Best to Work: Serenity on the Job

Ardagh, Arjuna. *The Translucent Revolution: How People Just Like You Are Waking Up and Changing the World*. Novato, CA New World Library, 2005.

Block, Peter. *The Answer to How Is Yes: Acting on What Matters*. San Francisco: Berrett-Koehlern Publishers, 2003.

Boldt, Laurence G. *Zen and the Art of Making a Living*. New York: Penguin Group, 1999.

Part Three: Serenity in the Storm

Muller, Wayne. *How, Then, Shall We Live? Four Simple Questions that Reveal the Beauty and Meaning of Our Lives*. New York: Bantam Books, 1996.

Chapter Nine: Serenity through Crisis and Change

Chopra, Deepak. *The Spontaneous Fulfillment of Desire: Harnessing the Infinite Power of Coincidence*. New York: Three Rivers Press, 2003.

Holmes, Ernest. *Creative Ideas: A Spiritual Compass for Personal Expression*. Burbank, CA: Science of Mind Communications, 2009.

Leonard, George. *The Way of Aikido: Life Lessons from an American Sensei*. New York: Penguin Group, 1999.

Tolle, Eckhart. *A New Earth: Awakening to Your Life's Purpose*. New York: Penguin Group, 2005.

Ueshiba, Morihei. *The Art of Peace*. Boston: Shambala Publications, 1992.

Watson, Lillian Eichler. *Light from Many Lamps*. New York: Simon & Schuster, 1951.

Chapter Ten: Saying Good-Bye: Loss, Death, and Rebirth

Anderson, Megory. *Sacred Dying: Creating Rituals for Embracing the End of Life*. : Prima Publishing, 2001.

Callanan, Maggie and Patricia Kelley. *Final Gifts: Understanding the Special Awareness, Needs, and Communications of the Dying*. New York: Simon & Schuster, 1992.

Campbell, Don. *Music: Physician for Times to Come*. Wheaton, IL: Quest Books, 1991.

Khan, Hazrat Inayat. *The Mysticism of Sound and Music: The Sufi Teaching of Hazrat Inayat Khan*. Boston: Shambhala, 1991.

Leonard, George. *The Silent Pulse: A Search for the Perfect Rhythm that Exists in Each of Us*. Salt Lake City: Gibbs Smith, 2006.

Murphy, Michael. *The Future of the Body: Explorations into the Further Evolution of Human Nature*. New York: Tarcher/Putnam, 1992.

Nearing, Helen. *Light on Aging and Dying*. Gardiner, ME: Tilbury House, 1995.

Music-Thanatology Association International
(website: www.mtai.org)

Chapter Eleven: Peace, Be Still: Serene Faith and Grace

Barker, Raymond Charles. *Treat Yourself to Life*. Camarillo, CA: DeVorss, 1996.

Brunton, Paul. *The Quest of the Overself*. New York: Random House, 2003.

Helminski, Kabir Edmund. *Living Presence: A Sufi Way to Mindfulness and the Essential Self*. New York: Tarcher/Perigree, 1992.

Tolle, Eckhart. *Oneness with All Life*. New York: Dutton, 2008.

Trine, Ralph Waldo. *In Tune with the Infinite*. Radford, VA: Wilder Publications, 2008.

Chapter Twelve: Celebrating Serenity All Year Round: A Collection of Practical Tips

Breathnach, Sarah Ban. *Simple Abundance: A Daybook of Comfort and Joy*. New York: Time Warner, 1995.

Moran, Victoria. *Younger by the Day: 365 Ways to Rejuvenate Your Body and Revitalize Your Spirit*. New York: HarperCollins, 2004.

Stoddard, Alexandra. *Living a Beautiful Life: 500 Ways to Add Elegance, Order, Beauty, and Joy to Every Day of Your Life*. New York: HarperCollins, 1986.

About the Author

Candy Paull is the author of *The Heart of Abundance*, *Finding Serenity in Seasons of Stress*, *The Translucent Heart*, *The Art of Simplicity*, *The Art of Abundance*, *The Art of Encouragement*, *Inner Abundance*, *The Most Wonderful Time of the Year*, and other books.

Candy is a freelance writer specializing in marketing materials for book publishers. She has owned her own business since 1990 and has also been a bookstore buyer and an advertising manager for a small publisher, for a total of more than thirty years' involvement in the publishing industry.

She is also a published songwriter and performer who makes her home in Nashville, Tennessee. Candy is known for her encouraging lifestyle, and her philosophy of life springs from her experiences as a writer and musician involved in a creative arts community. Her open approach to spirituality draws insight and wisdom from many spiritual traditions.

There is something inside each of us that is trustworthy, whole, and wise. Instead of always trying to "fix" what is "broken" in our lives, Candy Paull helps us experience the profound wholeness that lies at the center of the universe—and in our own human hearts.

Connect with Candy Online

website: www.candypaull.com
blog: http://candypaull.com/blog.htm

Books by Candy Paull

The Heart of Abundance
A Simple Guide to Appreciating and Enjoying Life
e-book © 2010, 2013 Candy Paull

    The Heart of Abundance is a free "best of" collection from Candy Paull's books. Discover more abundance, encouragement, and simplicity in your life. Be present, see the Divine at work in all circumstances, and experience ordinary life as sacred. Learn to practice the art of abundance as a form of spiritual awareness based in gratitude. Contains quotes, meditations, prayers, and instant inspiration.

The Artful Living Series

The Art of Abundance
A Simple Guide to Discovering Life's Treasures
© 1998, 2006 Candy Paull; e-book © 2010 Candy Paull
Originally published in 1998 by Honor Books
Second edition published in 2006 by Stewart, Tabori & Chang

    The Art of Abundance is not about greed or selfishness. *The Art of Abundance* is about celebrating life right now, this minute. It is a way of looking at the potential your life holds—the little blessings to be thankful for now and the gifts that God wants to give you, if you'll just open your heart to receive.

The Art of Encouragement
A Simple Guide to Living Life from the Heart
© 2003, 2006 Candy Paull; e-book © 2010 Candy Paull
Originally published in 2003 by Stewart House Publishers
Second edition published in 2006 by Stewart, Tabori & Chang

    Encouragement is the art of abundance shared and multiplied. It is a way of living that seeks to bless each person we meet. Encouragement is love in action. The art of encouragement is the art of creating community and celebrating friendship.

The Art of Simplicity
A Simple Guide to Focusing on the Essentials of the Heart
© 2006 Candy Paull; e-book © 2010 Candy Paull
Originally published in 2006 by Stewart, Tabori & Chang

Simplicity opens the way to the center of the heart—the still place where quiet, healing, and a still, small voice await. Simplicity is making elegant choices, treasuring precious moments, and valuing that which is of eternal worth. Simplicity is singleness of heart focused on the essentials of life rather than distractions caused by our desires and fears.

———————

The Translucent Heart
Inspired Choices for Challenging Times
e-book © 2013 Candy Paull

The Translucent Heart is a new collection of meditations and quotes for the spiritual journey. From listening to your inner guidance to discovering the sacred in ordinary life, *The Translucent Heart* offers devotional insights for more luminous living. Discover the joys of abiding in the light of Divine Love every day.

Inner Abundance
Affirmations for Confidence, Creativity, and Higher Consciousness
e-book © 2009 Candy Paull

Inner Abundance gently helps you discover your hidden potential to create a happier and more satisfying life. The meditations, quotes, and affirmations in this book remind you that true abundance is available every day, no matter what you may be going through.

31 Days of Abundance
Meditations to Help You Make the Most of Every Moment
e-book © 2010 Candy Paull

31 Days of Abundance offers a month's worth of inspirational thoughts, quotes, and practical actions that remind you to appreciate and embrace the gifts of life today.

31 Days of Encouragement
Meditations to Help You Persevere and Thrive in Difficult Times
e-book © 2010 Candy Paull

A month's worth of meditations encourage you to keep on keeping on, persevering through tough times to fashion a life that is meaningful to you and a blessing to the world.

31 Days of Simplicity
Meditations to Help You Live with Greater Joy and Serenity
e-book © 2010 Candy Paull

A month of practical advice, inspiring quotes, and daily meditations help you clear both outer and inner clutter, encouraging you to order your priorities around what matters most.

Christmas Abundance
A Simple Guide to Discovering the True Meaning of Christmas
© 2000 Candy Paull/Thomas Nelson Publishers

Christmas Abundance is a celebratory look at Christmas—from the small joys of the scents, sights, sounds, tastes, and textures of Christmas as we celebrate it today to the true meaning of Christmas in the birth of Christ.

Now available in e-book format from Thomas Nelson Publishers:

The Most Wonderful Time of the Year
101 Inspiring Ways to Enjoy Christmas
© 2009 Howard/Simon & Schuster

Along with inspirational meditations, you'll find quotes, scripture verses, and simple tips that help you choose easier ways to savor the season and make the most of every precious moment.

Special Thanks

- Gary Krebs: I honor your vision, your publishing skills, the way you discover and nurture talent. Thank you for including me in your magic circle.
- Steven Gladstone: Because you believe in me, anything is possible. I rely on your integrity and intelligence, but I love your heart the best.
- My family: Mom, Dad, Ellen, Lee, Ed: I love you more than words can tell. You have been my safe place, and you are heroes in my eyes. Thank you for believing through the dark times.
- Donna Michael: Dearest friend, inspiration, and wise counselor. You are music in my life.
- Karlen Evins: From lavender farm girl on Goatback Mountain to prayer partner, confidante, and encourager, you are my most amazing friend.
- Butterfly: Goddess Grandmother and spiritual mentor, you are so beautiful to me.
- Blue Heron and the Goddesses: Sweet sisters of harmony, chantemiah for the inspiration and the grounding.

- Dr. Mitch Johnson and the CSLN family: My spiritual home, the place of wise teaching and soulful community. Thank you for the love and the spirit of positive living.
- Skip Ewing: Songwriting hero, musical inspiration, and meditation teacher who helped me move into a deeper wisdom. Gratitude beyond words.
- Chuck Whiting: Cowriter, friend, and gentle inspiration. You are forever in my heart.
- Dwight Liles: Dear soul mate who can read my heart and put it to music. Friend, cowriter, conversationalist, mentor, and music maker extraordinaire.
- Many blessings to the Cultural Creatives who have been my Beloved Community—in Nashville and in Seattle. It would take a book to write all your names. Know that your courage and beauty are part of any creative work I do. I honor you with gratitude.

19794761R00132